A Caregiver's Survival and Personal Story...

# *But I Can Still Dance*

## Carleen Breskin Riach

ISBN 978-1-958678-09-1 (softcover)
ISBN 978-1-958678-10-7 (ebook)
Library of Congress Control Number: 2022912511

Printed in the United States of America.

Book Vine Press
2516 Highland Dr.
Palatine, IL 60067

This book is dedicated to the many caregivers in the world who keep dancing even though they can no longer hear the music.

# *Contents*

PART TWO: Practical Living

# *Preface*

BUT I CAN STILL DANCE is the story of the conquering of many sufferings and sorrows I encountered while caring for my husband as he lived through the shattering progression of Parkinson's disease. I tell of the ordeals with the hope that doing so may bring some measure of comfort and relief to others who are cast in the role of caregiver to a chronically ill person. Eventual victory over my difficulties makes me believe that others may do the same, benefiting from the experience of another person who has already trudged that path.

Financial strain, conquering guilt, depression, and the difficulties of day-to-day living with a physically disabled person are dealt with frankly in this narrative. I have been honest and candid in dealing with issues that usually are skirted in printed works such as this one. A forthright approach to coping with loneliness and lack of intimate companionship are a major part of the story. We live with frustrating and heart-wrenching circumstances when we live with a person passing through a stage of life marked by severe, inexorable transitions from health to sickness, with only one ending. Tough issues must be worked through if one is to maintain a life that is not devoid of hope. As the poet said, "Work without hope draws nectar in a sieve." The solutions are in this book.

You will see how we managed to balance the scale of our lives in an atmosphere of dignity and love. You will discover that the tools we developed for coping were forged on the anvil of despair with the hammer of desperation. In time these methods became principles that slowly transformed our lives from fear to peace and tranquility. What we learned gave our lives a dimension of acceptability, and made it possible for me, the caregiver, to achieve and maintain a level of equanimity.

As my duties stretched over a decade and a half, at times I felt I would never be free from what seemed like a servitude in prison. My life appeared to be over.

I was wrong. For in time, I was released from constant crisis and passed into a new phase of my life. I took with me a legacy of exquisite memories—treasures that could only be bestowed upon one who gave up a part of himself for someone else.

Perhaps you will also, my fellow caregiver. Key is knowing that you can create a happy life for yourself while still being a caregiver to a chronically ill person. And you will one day rejoice in recollections of the evolution from resentment to honest love, support, and finally total peace and gratification. I wish you Godspeed on your journey, and know that you are not alone.

# Acknowledgement

I want to thank Don Clarke for the help he gave me in the writing of this book. Most of all, I thank him for showing me I could keep dancing through the challenges that faced me when I thought I could not take one more step.

I'm also grateful to Chuck Riach for the encouragement he offered me in republishing BUT I CAN STILL DANCE.

This book could not have been written, and my journey could not have been travelled without the loving support of Chester Breskin's family, and my family and devoted friends.

# PART ONE

# 1

## The First Dance

### The First Response to the Illness

All over the world, television and radio broadcasts cried out details of a major crisis taking place in a faraway country. How ironic it was, while paying close attention to the blaring news reports, I was setting my own dinner table for our Thanksgiving celebration the following day. My mind shifted back and forth and settled on the immediate beauty before me. The delicate pink-and-gold china plates and the shiny silver utensils rested on a dainty lace tablecloth and reflected snowflakes of light onto the sparkling crystal goblets. The beauty before my eyes made me think how far removed I was from any insecurity. But as I listened to the radio my own state of well-being diminished and my sadness stirred for the hostages being held in Iran that very minute, knowing that they might never have Thanksgiving dinner with their loved ones again. I feared for the brave souls, including sixty Americans, captured by Islamic revolutionaries in the U.S. Embassy in Teheran twenty-three days earlier. Terrified for their lost freedom, I trembled, and consciously felt a deeper gratitude for my own personally restored peace this holiday season.

My thoughts continuously raced between my own reality and projected fear for the captives. One moment I was happy for myself, and the next moment I shuddered thinking of what it might be like being held hostage against my own free will. How strange, I thought, that some destinies are molded by colossal events that change lives all at once, and sometimes colossal changes in our lives can result simply from a subtle and slow-moving source.

Just then I once more focused on the exquisite Thanksgiving table. The beautiful carved wooden candlesticks that my husband, Chester and I had bought on our recent second honeymoon to the Orient seemed a symbol of security as they stood sentinel against the Los Angeles newscast screaming in the background. The Samurai warrior figures, mighty and colorful in their full regalia, held my attention at that moment, seemingly poised to protect me from any outside force.

At the time of this memorable Thanksgiving holiday in 1979, my husband, Chester and I were living in his condominium which was a part of the property settlement of our divorce the year before. We had entered the road of matrimony fifteen years earlier in 1964, madly in love with each other, with the best of intentions for a long and happy life together. However, through the years, our strong personality conflicts caused us to have problems that ultimately resulted in irreconcilable differences. Though it felt like pulling cement apart, because we really did greatly love and care for each other, we came to a place in our lives where we saw no other alternative but to live our lives separately.

Contrary to our plans, instead of moving on with individual lives, we found that our separate paths ultimately led us each to unbearable loneliness. Unhappy as we had previously been in our marriage, we experienced even a deeper pain in its dissolution. It was as if we had walked down the cold and desolate road of a new life with no shelter in sight, certainly not taking pleasure from the fancies we passed along the way. What was supposed to have been an expansion of our lives living separately, imagining that there would be greener pastures beyond our boundaries, turned out to be dark and dreary days with only memories of each other lighting the way. Instead of enjoying our lives individually, many disappointments in the disunion prompted us to see that perhaps the major mistake had not been in our marriage, but in our divorce. In calculating the things of real value, we found that our separate lives had been barren, and we knew our lives could only be worthwhile as the team we had been together, before our separation. We realized how precious was our love for each other and how much we had missed the life together we had grown accustomed to over the years that we had been married.

After that lonely and unhappy year, we were able to find the courage to set our pride aside and admit to ourselves and to each other that we could not make the divorce work. At the same time, it suddenly became clear that the error could be corrected by giving our marriage another sincere and earnest try. Once more we reached out for each other's hand as we rerouted our paths and searched for the way to return safely back home.

Needless to say, we felt saddened for the destruction the pending divorce had caused. In the turmoil we were forced to give up many things, including our lovely home in Los Angeles. However, the material sacrifices were but a small price to pay for the new and enthusiastic beginning encircling us at the time of our reconciliation. I was radiantly happy to be living again as Chester's wife, and I could likewise read clearly in his eyes the depth of the love he felt for me when he returned to my side as well. All at once the courage we needed to set aside our divorce appeared to be but a grain of sand compared to the mountains of happiness we knew we were going to build this time.

Now, to top it off, our entire families were planning to join us for Thanksgiving dinner with a special holiday celebration the next day. My cup ran over with gratitude. Even though I knew that Thanksgiving was a day for sharing, I felt that somehow this time, this holiday belonged to me!

So deep in thought was I at that moment that I could hardly hear the telephone ring over the blasting announcements on the radio. The receiver shook in my hand as I picked it up and held it to my ear. I was nervous and excited from the combination of events that occurred during the day. But most of all, I was gloriously happy for my own good fortune.

"Nancy, so glad you called." I was pleased to share my happiness with my friend. "My struggle is finally over. I'm once more home where I belong, and it feels wonderful to be back," I said. I took a very deep breath and sighed as I looked at the phone, waiting for my friend's response.

"That's really great. I'm happy for you too," she answered. "We all are" (meaning of course our friends.) Have a wonderful holiday with your family. Happy Thanksgiving."

"Thanks Nancy, a very happy Thanksgiving to you too."

I put the phone down and sat by the window, impatiently watching the cars go by as I waited for Chester's car to pull in the driveway. I felt so lucky to have my life's partner back by my side during this world crisis and I knew his strong arms and powerful spirit would somehow shield me from the dreadful events of the day. Even with all of the emotion the day's crisis brought forth, my mind mischievously wandered to thoughts of savagely and lustfully seducing my mate the second he walked in the door. I couldn't wait to see him, hold on tightly, and tell him that I was the luckiest woman in the world to have him for my husband.

I turned down the lights and lit the candles in my beloved carved candlesticks. Their flames delicately illuminated the room and gave off a peaceful, gentle aura adding an unusual warmth to the special setting. I was eager to surprise Chester with my excitement as we ushered in this very special Thanksgiving eve together. The sun had gone down, and evening had already settled in. The lovely scene was to have been a symbol of the beginning of our new and beautiful life together.

A long time passed since I put the phone down with Nancy. It seemed as if I had been waiting forever, and I didn't understand what might have detained Chester. It was most unlike him to come home late enough for the candles' flames to begin flickering in the twilight. Finally, I heard the key in the lock and the front door opened slowly. With my very first glance at him, it was clear that Chester's expressive green eyes did not display signs of joy. In fact, he looked strained, worried, and frightened. I knew something was wrong. Instead of falling into my arms with delight and pleasure, as I had expected him to do, he drew me close, and I could feel terror in his racing heart. He clung to me tightly.

"What's the matter?" I blurted out questions one after another. "Where were you? What happened? Are you all right? Why are you so late?" After just a few seconds, but what seemed to be an eternity, Chester finally managed to say the few words that would reshape our lives for our forever.

"I have Parkinson's disease," he said, holding back tears. "I've been at the doctor's office all afternoon." He sighed, and said, "He gave me all kinds of tests." Once more he took a deep breath, "He's sure."

His words were like knives being thrown at me. I wanted to dodge their targets. "Oh no, I can't believe it," I cried. I went on with more questions, "What does that mean? What is Parkinson's disease? Are you sure the doctor is certain?"

He whispered, "Yes, he's positive, absolutely sure."

His words quietly dwindled into silence. He was choked up and so was I. He just looked at me in a daze. I didn't know just what I should say or do, but the one thing that I did know was that his need for emotional support was more important than everything else around us. What I did not know on that Thanksgiving eve of 1979 was that nevermore were we to enjoy a peaceful mutual spirit in our storybook plans.

My Thanksgiving table lost meaning. It was all at once terribly insignificant. Even more astounding was the fact that the trembling I had for the hostages in Iran now appeared to be present for me. From that very moment, what I had feared so greatly for the captives in Teheran, in a bizarre way, happened in my own life.

Though I wasn't actually aware of the magnitude of the situation upon the first diagnosis of the illness, I ultimately did lose my freedom as I became, in a sense, a hostage to Chester's illness. It was as if a strange intruder crept into our lives and with just a few words uttered by Chester's doctor all of our wonderful plans were confiscated. I thought, "It was over before it began. We didn't even have a chance."

My mind rushed to panic and disbelief. Refusing to accept what I heard, I stubbornly clung to the thought that surely someday soon the doctors would find there had been an error. More than anything, however, I felt as if the film had abruptly, without warning, been yanked from a projector showing a beautiful scene of a peaceful and happy movie. When the sight and sound returned, the plot had been changed to an ominous and frightening picture.

I didn't know much about Parkinson's disease then, but I did know enough to feel scared for both of us, and as the days went by, I found there was a myriad of genuinely frightening questions that had no real answers. I couldn't believe that so many doctors could come up with the same few comments that really didn't make any sense at all, "A slow-moving illness with no cure; only a limited degree of relief to the symptoms, and they will progressively get worse as time goes on."

During my early investigation into the illness, I learned that Chester's symptoms would progress until, finally, he would be completely dependent on another person. Eventually, he would be confined to a wheelchair or bed, and he would need assistance with his normal bodily functions besides losing the strength to speak, eat, and to think normally. What we were offered was a race against time before Chester would become frail, sickly, and demented. Not a pretty future to view.

No matter how much we begged for a reversal in the diagnosis, hoping beyond hope for an error, the decision was the same. There was no error.

Though we certainly had our problems in the past, including separation the year before, we had always been able to find solutions for each one and overcome our difficulties. Coming out of them somewhat scarred, we were strong and willing to continue life's journey together.

We also managed to find the right combination to coexist peacefully with each other's families. My son was five years old when we first married in 1964, and my husband's daughter and son were eight and eleven. At our reconciliation in 1979, they were grown, and we all had some serious soul-searching and honest feelings to uncover with one another. Not long after our reconciliation we all became close friends. We lived through life as long as we had control, and the result was always the same. There had always been a beginning, a middle, and an ending for each problem—that was the nature of life. But somehow this test felt different. A peaceful ending was not in sight.

My first thought was for Chester. At the time of the Parkinson's diagnosis he was in the prime of his life, a vibrant, handsome, and successful man with guts and panache. I wondered how all of this would change him. How badly would he be hurt and demoralized? I was frightened imagining that his goals and plans would be thwarted while an ever-present, lurking threat of deterioration hung in the background of his future. I sadly pondered, would he have to go through what the doctors had coldly described, "a most serious and difficult life with no alternate course"?

My mind raced wildly into irrational oblivion, finally striking a most sensitive cord. With no doubt to hang on to, I shared the thoughts of pain Chester would endure with the imminent collapse of his health. I couldn't help wonder how the illness would also affect my life and how it would complicate our lives as a couple. We were two strong, energetic, vital individuals, and we had both worked hard to arrive at a place in life that mingled our mutual goals. But instead of dreaming about the wonderful days filled with happy plans and ideas for our new lives together, what unfolded for us was a stressful life punctuated with worry and anxiety. We were faced with the probability that one day Chester would be in a wheelchair or confined to bed, needing assistance for his every basic physical and mental need. These thoughts tortured me as I sought, with outward calm, to soothe my husband's shaken morale. At the same time I muffled the shrieks of agony that fought to escape from my own aching heart.

How odd that the next week after this Thanksgiving holiday we were scheduled to formally and legally nullify our previously begun divorce. I remember sitting quietly and thinking about the pending appointment with our attorney. I knew, however, that no choice was involved, nor would my plans be altered. I knew that I would continue to stand firmly at my husband's side and remain his loving wife and friend. Instinctively, I also knew that if the draw had been in reverse that his decision would have been to stay with me. In fact, I recalled at that moment a point in time fifteen years before.

Although my visions of the future were cloudy, it was clear that we had come a very long way in our marriage. Thus, without fully knowing how it would be done, I felt certain that we would somehow find the means to surmount the gigantic hurdle that now faced us, too. Without knowledge of the scope of what was to lie ahead, I ventured forward and got ready for our very first dance.

# 2

## *The Music Stopped*

### *Shock and Grief*

It was quiet and still. I felt as if I had become a spectator in a new level of existence that was suddenly assigned to me. A cold, deathlike aura now encompassed my life within this new-sprung, chilling environment.

This was my first lesson in watching the most painful death of all, the slow demise of another's inner being; it was the beginning of many significant revelations that were to follow. In this new passage of life I learned the importance of being aware of life as it truly is, and how really vulnerable, and yet at the same time so strong, is a human being.

Even though the sky of an Indian summer and the rich hues of late autumn were warm and golden, my body felt cold, my hands numb and icy. The pleasing aroma and the darting sounds of firewood crackling in the fireplace had always guaranteed warmth and stability before. So how was I to know that now the colorful tinges that illuminated the room would merely become symbols of the last moments of inner peace that I would feel for many years to come? The transition of twilight dividing the day's light and the night's darkness seemed to now divide the moods between my accustomed stable form of security and this frightening jolt of reality lurking in the background.

A state of balance left my life as I constantly tried to conceal my deep sadness. No matter how intensely I tried to hide from what was happening, and no matter how vehemently I sought to create a cheerful existence, I just could not overcome my own feelings that came from my husband's recent diagnosis of Parkinson's disease. My world became an impossible maze begging for a solution. All the while, and no matter which way I went, I still was forced to live in this deep bed of sadness.

I did not know then that what I thought felt like pain was actually grief. I grieved for the happy way of life that I thought would last forever, and I grieved for the future as I stood witness to the blasting of our hopes and dreams. While I watched my rapport with Chester slip away, I grieved for the closeness of the dear companion and friend that had been killed by the process of the disease. I grieved for the loss of sexual fantasies that I knew would never again be acted out, and I grieved for the loss of dawns breaking with great awakenings together, knowing we would never again watch the sun's first rays, holding on tightly as selfish lovers. I grieved with the ache of watching a loved one suffer, and I felt my own heart collapse for fear of the days ahead for myself. No matter how hard I tried, it seemed almost impossible to close the door on grief, move on past the oblivion that it laid out, and continue to the next phase of life.

However, we did survive those first days, and then the next stage of the grief process occurred, culminating in deep distress. And oh, how the pain did hurt. The lessons continued mercilessly. I learned how it felt to really hurt with no sign of a cure for the ailing inner bruises. Through the window of our incarceration we could see life continuing normally for the rest of the world, but without warning it seemed that we were singled out for our own special bolt of lightning. Everything around us that had so recently appeared vibrant and exciting, which had helped us reconcile our marriage just a short time before, appeared now to come to a screeching halt.

From the very first day we learned of this frightening burden— things were different. Our regained bliss and all of our happy images had been removed by this sudden turn in our lives, and with it the joyous plans to rebuild and restore our divorce-ridden and withered relationship had disappeared as well. Suddenly our new-found Camelot vanished. The fantasies making up what we expected to be our future were blown away in an instant like twigs from a tree caught in a sudden windstorm. Instead of exploiting a strong and confident position, the focus had now shifted to just getting through the shock of the death of our beautiful dreams. Now rather than moving through the steps of the graceful routine of life we thought we knew, we began to carefully scrutinize Chester's every movement and search for abnormalities in his behavior every day.

It is strange that just a short time before this period, we had exuberantly launched the beginning of our reconciliation by going on a second honeymoon to Japan. We watched the cherry blossoms bloom with an unusual beauty that happy springtime prior to the fateful Thanksgiving eve. The exultation of rekindled love for each other, along with a healthy appreciation for our individual selves, gave us cause for great celebration of total happiness on this trip.

We reveled in that exciting adventure and made friends of strangers who were our companions in those foreign lands. We experienced the frivolity of youth restored and a vitality to seek the real essence of each day. We held hands and kissed in public in the bright sunlight of morning, and looked at each other with the warmth and tenderness that only honeymooners have as they electrify one another with their final gaze of evening. A gigantic statue of Buddha looked down on us as we clung to each other feeling a humility and deep respect for the ancient Asian culture. Discovering new joys as we playfully investigated the beautiful Japanese spas, we giggled like teenagers while we bathed together practicing the tradition of the land. Learning to eat with chopsticks made each meal a grand event truly worthy of Japanese customs. We sauntered down floral paths and over dainty bridges in picturesque gardens, devouring the beauty of the exquisite treasures of Japan. Complete ecstasy.

"You two can't be married for fourteen years," a tour companion remarked, finding it difficult to believe we were so in love. "Nobody carries on like you two."

"Of course we have," I said, as I openly squeezed Chester's hand, not going into everything that made up the last fourteen years.

"We've been so blessed with our love and happiness," Chester offered. Then went on, "We're the luckiest two people in the world," and leaned over and kissed me on the cheek, not giving our new friends any of the details. All the same, we had great fun letting them think that we had always been that happy. It was so totally perfect, it almost seemed like it had been that way forever.

Though it seemed impossible, the perfection we felt when we flew home from that enchanted holiday disappeared just a few months later. It was as if our joyful thoughts had been tossed among the billowy white clouds outside the plane's little window. How strange it was that the wonderful experiences we had just enjoyed suddenly seemed but an illusory dream. Little did I know, drifting into a starry slumber on our return flight home, that as I snuggled close and buried my head on Chester's chest, the vibrations of the jet engines would lull me into one of the last peaceful sleeps that I would have for many years. I felt a safety, thinking that at long last I could count on my tomorrows, and that our future would be the product of a past built from glorious experiences like this one. Not for an instant did I think that the memories of the delicate sights and sounds of the Kabuki still dancing in my mind were to be the last gentle recollections in the peacetime of our lives. I felt Chester's strong arm around my shoulder as I lay my head back on the small airline pillow, and I clearly remembered him holding me tightly as we danced our last dance together on that happy second honeymoon adventure. He noticed that a few strands of my long blonde hair were moist as he stroked my cheek, and realizing that I had been weeping, he whispered, "Why are you crying, sweetheart? What's the matter?"

I looked up at his secure, confident face and meekly answered, "Tears of joy, darling. I'm so happy, I never want this trip to end." He hugged me.

In a hushed tone he murmured, "This trip may end, dear, but we will always be this happy."

Without warning, the music stopped, and I wondered what happened to "always." Within a matter of a few months, those gentle, safe moments abruptly gave way to the war zone in our minds. The serene images of delicate Japanese tea houses surrounded by softly dancing waterfalls in lush gardens were replaced by the harsh sounds of battles fought within our brains, and a combination of shock, grief, and pain became intertwined with our everyday state of being. As battle-scarred soldiers, we eventually had to settle into an acceptance of our grief.

It is peculiar that merely the words of the physical diagnosis could have so drastically changed our lives, while at the same time the progression of the illness moved at a relatively slow pace. Once the diagnosis was made, we nervously waited for each stage of the illness to follow, and they surely did! The inexorable march of Parkinson's disease then became our total obsession. We talked about little else, and when we weren't discussing the "what ifs" of the matter, we were thinking about it. We awoke each morning with the illness and the symptoms of it on our minds, and we went to sleep at night feeling the desperation of the situation before we eventually slid into our own individual nightmares. Our lives were now cut with new facets and we were no more to live a normal life. We had completely lost control.

When Chester's illness was discovered, we had many aspirations in our second chance at life together. I was just past 40 years old and strong and healthy since I was a regular tennis player. Chester was a bright and intelligent person with a quiet, keen wit, and though nearly 20 years my senior, he was a striking and sophisticated man. He had always taken great pride in his looks, perhaps even to the point of chic arrogance. He was even a bit conceited about his physical appearance and achievements in life. Though not of an extremely large build, he was debonair and in wonderful physical condition as a result of playing tennis every day himself for several years preceding his illness. The exercise in the California sunshine gave him a healthy tanned look and kept his body in excellent shape. He had been methodical and scientific about his tennis as well as everything else he undertook, and was deserving of the pride he took of his manifold accomplishments. Though he was strong and sure of himself, well put together physically and dynamic in the professional world, he still managed to maintain the quality of a quiet, gentle man with admirable humility.

For many years into the illness we enjoyed playing tennis together. In fact, we continued to play for a long time as the illness wound its way into our lives, giving up only when the Parkinson's symptoms caused Chester to suffer serious falls on the tennis court. Before our reconciliation and his acquiring the illness we had played a competitive game, and it was a major activity for us as partners. However, toward the end of his active mobility I became strikingly aware that we were "winners" by simply being able to play together one more time. Indeed, what a sad day it was for him when he played his last set. His final accident was one that we could not ignore. I watched him trip, stumble, and fall. He slid across the court on his face, then lay there helplessly covered in blood.

"Oh no! Oh nooo!" he screamed, as he fell to the ground.

I clutched his hand and knelt down beside him trying to shield his body from further pain. "You'll be all right Chester," I said, trying to encourage him, knowing full well that he would not.

A woman ran onto the court to see what happened. She pushed herself through the half a dozen or so people that crowded around, and looked at Chester.

"Thank God," she cried. "Someone said there was an accident. I thought it was my Bill."

I stared at her in disbelief.

Little did I know that was a sample of the lack of empathy we were to receive in the years that would follow. As we waited for the paramedics to come I thought to myself, "Poor Chester. What now?" I knew the deepest hurts would lie ahead. Tennis may seem like a small thing to give up—after all, it's only a game. But as an avid tennis player, it was an important part of Chester's life, and it was something he still could do within a fairly normal social context. But when he was forced to discontinue the game, it began the lengthy series of "I cant's" that he would eventually have to live with.

His professional career had been meaningful and successful. Chester was able to retire from a full-time occupation at an early age due to his keen business sense which led him to wise investments. He enjoyed a full life, and he was also fortunate in crucial decisions to arrive at the right place at the right time. Aside from a formal music education leading to a successful career as a musician in the big bands, he built a strong real estate investment business using only the knowledge he learned "on the streets." This actually gave him the attractive combination of a cultural and artistic background along with a savvy gained by natural instinct. During his working years, he had also built a profitable decorating and import business which had taken him to distant shores. Here was a man who was self-educated and eminently successful; a man of refinement, stature, looks, and class. At that point in life, he certainly had it all.

Our lives were rich in many areas. We were once more enjoying our friendships with those we had been forced to give up during our separation and we were happy to be back among mutual friends again. At last, our social life seemed relaxed and we were happy once more. More than anything we were having fun watching our families rejoin with a bold and happy spirit. Family parties were joyous events, since we, as well as our children, experienced those precious moments with greater appreciation than before our separation. We took honest and courageous steps to solve whatever difficulties existed among us before our reconciliation, and we were careful to leave no ambiguous feelings when we reunited as a family unit. We seriously engaged in honest talks with one another, ironing out all of our apparent differences and finding mature and workable solutions for our problems. All in all, we were vitally motivated with a challenging repertoire of activities with our family and friends.

Enjoying the expansion of our lives during this reconciliation period, we also felt the excitement of the reacquaintance of each other's bodies along with a deeper penetration into each other's souls. Before our divorce we had experienced an exciting and lustful relationship, and felt a physical and sexual passion for one another that continued throughout the entire time of our separation. But we buried these keen physical and emotional pleasures the very day that Parkinson's was discovered. We closed this entire, crucial chapter in our lives and the grief then became the master of our bedroom.

Ironically, for some time and in many ways, lovemaking took on a grander beauty by our having the courage to discover new forms of pleasure for each other. Just holding on to one another and staying very close produced a rebuttal of its own against the terrible grief that we were to finally endure. So, we held on to each other a little tighter, and had each other a little more, for just a little longer. Somehow when I felt Chester's gentle hands stroke my body and heard him whisper, "I love you," a new level of feeling was reached. Each word and caress was deep and important. Ecstasy still burned in our hearts.

Unfortunately, the grief that I felt from the inception of the illness eventually conquered my strengths, and I fell into a powerless state. Without warning, I was cut off from a way of life that I thought was mine, and in no way was I ready to release all that I had envisioned. However, ready or not, I could not stop the onset of the disintegration of the life that I had planned.

As in the ending of any fruitful relationship, the deepest losses are the thoughts of what the future may have held. When we reconciled in 1979, our hopeful fantasies seemed to be nearer and more realistic to us than our presently unfolding fate. But after a few short months of living with the illness, I had to wrestle with unknown fears and watch them take on their own reality. On our trip to the Orient, the future had looked so wonderfully inviting, and I could not wait for each new day. Now anxiety made me want to retreat to a place within myself. Unconsciously, I tried to free myself from the maze of confusion that surrounded me. As events unfolded, I became accustomed to one loss and adjusted to the life it produced. Then a new deprivation reduced it again, and something else was removed from what I thought was to be our adjusted life style. Although I was observing the disintegration of portions of my own life, I am sure that the greatest sadness and tragedy of all was to watch the man that I loved being reduced to a fraction of the person that he once was. It happened almost systematically, and very slowly. It was as if a craftsman disassembled a complicated mechanical doll, piece by piece, until the figure ceased working.

A myriad of thoughts have run through my mind regarding the beginning of this nightmare. I wonder if I had been wise enough to relax and coast along with the inevitable life changes that were occurring, would I have been more fully accepting of each current condition as it happened. Perhaps if I had better reconciled myself to our ultimate destinies, the wheel of our fortune may not have appeared so frightening. Or if I could only have just sat patiently and accepted each day, I might have seen that the alterations were not always of a magnitude consistent with my terrified illusions. The pity of it was, that as we waited for the symptoms to worsen, there was a real and substantial life there for us to enjoy on our journey together while Chester was still functioning in a stable manner.

Instead, I tried to fight the inevitable and pretend that all was normal, while at the same time I fearfully projected the progression of his illness. Realistically, my acceptance of reality and the healing process could not be completed without the phase of recognizing the grief for what it was. In spite of this, at the time, I was simply bogged down with the intense shock, along with the grief that shock produced. I was just plain scared and could not examine rationally any sensible alternatives to my feelings and reactions.

In the very difficult early stages of the illness, I appeared normal to the rest of the world since I kept my real feelings locked behind closed doors as though there were some deep shame involved with the illness. But my charade only prolonged the sadness that blocked my reaching a healthier and happier manner of living. Until one arrives at a point of total honesty in his life, the cover-up can be horrifyingly painful.

Grief is such an elusive state. You can't see it nor touch it, but oh, how you can feel it! You can deny that it is there, as I did; you can try to race over it quickly, as I did; you can think you will not feel it, as I did. But until you come to the realization that you have suffered a major loss from real changes in your life, you will not be ready to enter the next stage of recovery and begin to live without being afraid of the future. Once I finally recognized the damaging effects of the deep loss for such an extremely significant part of my life, things began to fall into place, and I was able to face each situation with a healthier perspective. Sometimes blind faith is all that is available. In essence I found there were alternatives to defeat, but no alternatives to reality. Ironically, the fears in my mind were much worse than the realities that eventually prevailed.

One of the saddest parts of a loss having to do with a chronic illness such as this is that not only is the healthy person forced to watch the decline and suffering of a dear loved one, but the quality of the caregiver's own life is greatly diminished. These self losses are of a magnitude beyond calculation. Somehow, no matter how badly one feels for another closely bonded individual, the most intense sorrow can be for the frustration in watching one's own life pass by while still strong and healthy. No matter how much compassion, love and admiration I had for my husband, the frightening feeling of "what will happen to me?" remained in the background on the canvas of our lives we were painting. I was desperately sad for this recognition.

Though the feelings of grief were intensely painful at times, the deepest pain became the impetus for a thorough acceptance of the situation and the positive life experiences that I was to enjoy later. To cope, I had to accept at last the realities before me. I had to allow myself to be thrust entirely into the midst of my problems, find my way through them, and acknowledge my pending future while not paying heed to the feeling that the music in our lives had suddenly stopped.

# 3

## Only the Slow Dances

### Ashamed of the Illness

The chain of events, that followed the discovery of Chester's illness, though they seemed appropriate at the time, were in fact extremely irrational and emotionally harmful to both of us. The heavy grief that we experienced gave way to withdrawal, which engendered indescribable feelings of embarrassment. It felt like shame; it prompted me to act as if I were ashamed; and thus, I knew, for no rational reason, I was ashamed of the illness. This thought, coupled with the fear of once more losing the way of life that we had recovered in our reconciliation, including friends, family, and a general normal lifestyle, finally culminated in an unreasonable guilt which prevented me from talking about the illness to anyone. I was obsessed with the illness, and at the same time tried to hide that I thought we were now different from everyone else. Concealment was all I had to keep me amongst the many, rather than speaking out and risking being alone and separate from the world I so terribly wanted to rejoin. Though I was aware this thinking was irrational, my survival seemed to depend upon rebuilding the walls I recently began to tear down. I felt desperately alone during our separation, even though I knew that I had my friends and family for support. This time, however, I had felt that I had no one with whom to confide. I couldn't even commiserate with Chester as my real feelings were concealed from him since I wanted to protect his feelings. Not enough time had elapsed in our reconciliation for our mutual trust to be rebuilt—it all happened so fast and seemed so unfair. One minute we were joyfully launching our future lives together on a second honeymoon, and then, without notice, our dreams had been seized from us. We had needed more time, and just when we began to be intimate confidants, we shut down helplessly from one another. I simply could not discuss my sad feelings with Chester, and there seemed no other alternative but to withdraw. I believed once more that the crisis was all mine, and no matter how hard I tried to reach out to either Chester or my friends, I felt alone. Separate. Ashamed. Not only was I ashamed of the illness, I was, more than anything, ashamed of myself for fostering these feelings. I felt completely immoral for the uncontrollable embarrassment I felt. And the worst part of all was that at a time when my loved one was understandably entrenched in his own agony, I thought, "Why can't I be there emotionally with him? We must fight together. We're one team now."

I wanted to be one with him, because I loved Chester dearly. But the door between me, him, and the world slammed shut with a silent but powerful, absolute force. The irony is that only a few months earlier when we reconciled, I could not wait to rejoin the world as "a couple" and to emerge again into public life, interacting with the community as involved human beings.

Our marriage certainly had had its own severe maladies associated with it, but somehow I felt as if they were always within my control. We could, and did, do something to correct them. The situation had ended well, and though the road had been tough enough to travel, the hard part was over, and the mere fact that our problems were conquered allowed me to at last relax and enjoy life. However, no matter what we did this time, we could not control the progression of Chester's illness, and we had to lie helplessly in wait at the mercy of the hideous symptoms. This was the first time that I realized that we did not have control.

This disappointment was then too great a burden for me to bear, as the decline of our newly found happiness appeared, in my own mind, as a nullification of our previous victories. Our lives looked to me a calamity, and even though I chose to stand by Chester, intellectually knowing that there was nothing to be ashamed of, I still felt embarrassed and ashamed. The reality was that Parkinson's disease was to be very much a part of our lives, and was the theme that created the atmosphere for the rest of our days together.

Quite simply the illness made us feel different when I wanted to be like everyone else. I wished that I could have slid back into the notch we had left and resume our proud and happy lifestyle much the same as it was just prior to Chester's illness. I hoped that the world wouldn't see the changes, but of course as the illness did not go away, the world eventually did notice, and we had to get used to the idea that we really were different.

Inevitable changes occurred in our lives, and defining the methods to face these changes were crucial. Some of them were automatic and casual; the alterations were simple and meant merely a passing into a less rigorous lifestyle. However, as the disease evolved, the adjustments took courage and we had to accept limitations to our lifestyle for which we were not ready. Many questions without answers faced us, that is, unless we resigned ourselves to total surrender. Acceptance is an extremely fragile condition and it had to be handled carefully. There had to be a distinction between the expectations and dreams that were relinquished and what hopes could be saved for our own new identity as we emerged to fight this challenge. I had to acknowledge my own part in this relationship and not be quick to give up the right to my own self in the process of realizing Chester's pain. Concessions had to be made regarding the realities of our marriage, but it was destructive for me to play victim when I could have risen and still fought for whatever dances were left for us to enjoy.

It is difficult to discern if the feelings of shame brought on the feelings of inferiority, or if the feelings of inferiority produced the awful shameful effects. Notwithstanding which came first, I had to deal with both. Whatever self-worth I had recouped during our reconciliation seemed to have vanished, and I was once more left with a shell devoid of confidence. The weight of the shame bent me deeply. Before, I used to enjoy tossing my long blond hair back and forth as I held my head high, walking with a pleasant, confident pace. How swiftly that attitude changed when the burden grew. My tempo slowed and dragged, as sounds do when a record is playing on an old fashioned wind-up phonograph when it is just about to die.

After a short time, Chester sought assistance from a psychiatrist who helped him get over his initial shock. I did not get help for a very long time, and as a result of my denial, I found out the hard way that his Parkinson's disease became a family illness. I believe I know now what Hippolytus Euripides meant in 428 B.C. when he said, "It is better to be sick than to attend the sick." I was faced not only with the burden of caring for Chester's needs, but also had to look past his pain and deal with my own life changes that his illness brought forth. I found that the well person sometimes actually takes on various qualities of the sick. When I went to the Parkinson's disease support groups, I sadly noticed that it was often difficult to see who was the caregiver and who was the person afflicted with the physical illness, as they look so much alike after a long period of caregiving. I had to learn to care for two people, myself and Chester—a most difficult task.

Before Parkinson's had taken its toll, Chester had a natural charisma which set him apart from the average man, and his sophistication and handsome appearance made me feel the envy of every other woman. He was known for immaculate taste in his clothing and wore his shirt collar starched and open under a variety of beautiful sport coats, always in the latest style. His well-coordinated outfits contrasted with his perfectly groomed, silver-gray hair, and he always looked as if he just stepped out of a men's fashion magazine. He had a confident manner that would make me melt when I saw him, and when we entered a room together I sensed that we were noticed for our striking appearance as a couple. We looked like we were "on top of the world," and this seemed to be the happiest time in my life. Then, apparently without warning, all of those wonderful feelings of pride disappeared and were replaced by deep emotional discomfort.

At the beginning, I thought if we didn't mention Chester's illness, then nobody would notice it. But before long, as his symptoms progressed there were many intrusive questions which demanded explanations.

"Why doesn't Chester smile anymore? Is he unhappy again? Whatever is the matter with him?" a friend asked me one day.

"Is Chester moody again like he was during your separation? He doesn't look well. Is his health okay?" a relative asked after a tiring family get-together.

On a trip, our tour guide asked me, "Is Chester walking slowly and tripping because he's tired? Is he ill? Is it too hard for him to keep up with the group?"

How badly I wanted to scream "Yes, yes, yes!" But silent resentment was my only reply.

Undoubtedly, the worst comment of all was from a tennis buddy of his. One day Chester came home from the tennis club upset. He had tears in his eyes. Instinctively I knew what happened.

"They told me I couldn't play with the guys anymore. I can't run fast enough," he said. "What should I do"?

"I don't know," I answered, again, "I just don't know." But I did know. It was time for explanations.

The physical effects had now started to become apparent. Chester no longer smiled because his facial muscles were affected, and he was left with a waxy expression on his once ever-so-handsome face. He was slow and tired because the illness was beginning to show, and his feet could not raise up fast enough for a normal step. And before long it was clear that he could only dance the very slow dances.

"What right did the world have to invade our lives?" I thought. "How insensitive were people who didn't seem to care that we might be hurt."

Sorrowfully, however, the most audacious of insensitivities were from my own feelings. I was used to Chester a certain way, and as time went on and his symptoms advanced, I was embarrassed by the changes in how he looked, talked, and acted. Even though my heart broke for him, as he changed physically and mentally I could not handle the explanations in a mature and stable manner. I realize now that no one set out to injure either of us, and perhaps my sensitivities were simply exaggerated by my own shame and guilt. A difficult dilemma, indeed.

How could I love someone, be filled with great admiration and desire for the person, and still be ashamed of him? I didn't understand my feelings and in a way almost felt that I deserved the guilt that I felt. I had been proud of my morals and basic integrity in choosing to return to the marriage knowing of Chester's illness. I was sure that these loyal and noble deeds did not stem from martyrdom; they simply were the result of being part of a family and caring about the welfare of my husband. The difficult part was that at the same time I selfishly wanted to have a normal life. I was so confused. No matter how vigorously I tried to cover up the realities I could not make Chester act as he did before he became ill. How badly I wished that I could be known as just Chester's wife again, without an additional explanation when we were introduced to people. I desperately desired to wake up one morning and find it had all been a bad dream. But instead the nightmare continued, and my feelings of isolation remained. I felt as if I were on an island in the center of the busy world with only my new-found loneliness for a companion. I wondered if I would ever be able to deal with the transformation that had taken place and continue to live completely once again. Many moments were spent fantasizing that we were walking down the boulevard in the sunshine, holding hands and feeling the sun warming them, together.

The years of my solitude crept by, and finally, after twelve years of dealing with this inner struggle, in 1991 a crucial turning point occurred for me. I admitted to myself that I strongly missed having someone that I could honestly talk to, confide in, and count on, and that I could not tolerate the silence in our lives anymore. I realized that I had to decide how and if I would live my life. Yes, *my* life. I recognized that I had one, too. I knew there must be a way for our two lives to blend with harmony for us both to enjoy our own lives, and at the same time, still support each other's needs. Mainly I grasped that all anyone has, is time. I also hoped that somehow each of us would find a pleasure in knowing that our soulmate might find a joy in life's neverending learning process.

I realized that I was not selfish in my thoughts for my own emotional survival. At last, I had hopes for a measure of quality in my life that could no longer be overlooked. The need to experience a fulfilled life caused me great discomfort and frustration, as I knew I had allowed the opportunity of living to lie dormant for too long. Perhaps Chester's outstanding spirit and determination gave me the strength to have the courage I needed for my own sustenance through the years, but now I recognized the responsibility to life itself. Chester seemed to be able to live his life realistically and accept his limitations as they grew, and he taught me that we must all live our lives to the fullest measure that is possible. At this time, twelve years later, I understood that Chester's capabilities were different from mine. It became clear that I must give back to the world whatever my own capacity was for living, and that I must find a way to cease merely existing. There came a time when it was as impossible for me to try to live my life within the confines of Chester's abilities as it was for him to live within mine.

Many times during the course of the sixteen years of Chester's illness people complimented me on my ability to stay in my marriage and "hang in there." I never understood the basis for this admiration. For me, there never was an option. Leaving and walking away was simply not an option; my dilemma stemmed from the unanswered questions of how to live in the confines of caregiver and not give away my own entire right to live. Eventually I learned that the long-term caregiver does not tend an illness, but instead adjusts to it and adapts to life around her.

In 1992, thirteen years into Chester's illness, we celebrated 28 years of marriage with a wedding anniversary celebration. To enjoy this important event in our lives, I took Chester to a beautiful hotel overlooking the ocean down the coast of Southern California. I felt pride in taking care of him myself as we spent a couple of days together. We talked, reflected, and enjoyed each other as we watched the majestic sunsets shimmering on the vast Pacific ocean, and at twilight we held hands and listened to the music playing softly in the background. I'm sure that one of the highlights of my life will be to remember how proud I felt to be with him and to show the world that he was my husband. I will never forget the happiness I felt when I noticed how extremely handsome he still looked with his stunning head of white hair, dressed in immaculate taste, with his starched collar and beautiful sport coat, when I wheeled him in his wheelchair into the elegant restaurant in the hotel.

"A table for two, please," I said. I went on proudly, "We prefer to be seated next to the dance floor. We enjoy watching the dancers."

The matre d' nodded kindly and showed us to our table. As we listened to the music, we held hands tightly and kept time with our eyes and our hearts. It didn't seem to matter at all that we weren't on the dance floor because we were gloriously slow dancing in our reverie.

# 4

# It Takes Two to Tango

## Living in a Couple's World

Doors suddenly slammed shut. Though there was no printed word, it was as if I saw an imaginary sign above many entrances reading "Couples Only." No longer was I comfortable entering doorways that opened wide for me in the past, nor did I fully understand the new unwritten rules and the reasoning behind these new strange customs.

One of the most difficult concepts for me to accept was the distinction between having a normal social life as husband and wife, and being denied social contacts individually while being a caregiver to a husband who could no longer participate on a normal social level. Everyone has the need and desire to feel a part of his own world, and I was no longer able to fit the slot I previously occupied in the world that I thought was mine. Although I was sympathetic with Chester's feelings, my own emotions, worn from frustration, were shredded. When I dared look at reality, I saw the cold facts: Our previous life was led as a couple in a world where you require a partner to dance when the music begins.

During the years since Chester's illness began, feelings of rejection from our friends grew. I felt unwanted and had difficulty coping with the mixed messages they sent. I didn't know how to change the situation, yet one thing I did know was that I was very much married without a partner. Feeling extremely sensitive at this time and still remaining very close to Chester, as he was still totally my ally and best friend, I noticed a vast difference in the kinds of people around us. There was a strong contrast between the "devoted" and the "casual" friendships in our lives. And devoted as we were to each other, I still felt the desire for some casual social interaction with other people, as we had before with our acquaintances. However, our casual friends became condescending and patronizing, and the infrequent invitations from these friends seemed somewhat false and contrived. Though occasionally we received an invitation as a couple, for the most part it usually contained shades of obligation. Persist as we did, the effort to participate in the couples' world became increasingly more difficult for Chester, even though he was not yet completely bereft of social skills. In fact, Chester was bright and intelligent much of the time, and since he had been a talented professional musician, his artistic senses were highly developed as well. He had a sensitivity that musicians especially seem to feel, and also had training in classical and jazz to round out his repertoire of musical knowledge. He knew more about the arts than most of our casual friends, and was a worthwhile conversationalist in many subjects, when he could speak normally.

Though self-taught, he was well read and had strong, well-formed opinions on business and politics. Having been extremely successful in his economic enterprises when still alert and healthy, many people came to him for advice. Several things he touched became lucrative endeavors and he had been quick to react to whatever presented itself in his path. He had "chutzpah" and had been fearless in his personal business. Therefore, because he had been wise in a worldly manner, he possessed a remarkable strength and natural charisma.

Thus, all of these qualities enabled him to draw from strong mental resources when afflicted with the incapacitating aspects of Parkinson's disease. When he was aware and mentally nimble, he could be sharpwitted, humorous and quite conscious of life around him. In fact, he could still make me laugh with his very clever, dry sense of humor. However, the fact remained that his illness left him slow and very quiet, and often his dear and precious remarks went sadly unnoticed by those in his company. It almost seemed as if he were using English as a second language. He understood what was going on around him, but the conversation could not go beyond a superficial level, at a pace consistent with one concentrating on translation of the language itself. By the time the subject matter in a conversation reached his brain, was comprehended, digested, and a response prepared for the idea at hand, a new thought was already presented to him for which to rally. The pace of general conversation was simply too swift for his capable response. Unconsciously, by this time his companions had mentally left him behind. It's almost as if the channels on the dial seemed to turn quicker than the words he could get out. Though he understood what was happening, except to the very devoted, it appeared that he did not. It was as if he was never quite able to bring the baton to the head of the line in a relay, so he just hung back of the crowd.

Finally, I did come to terms with these issues, and I'm relieved that I found a few "devotees" in our corner; however, at the time of these discoveries we had to endure a lot of serious emotional pain. Throughout this period of adjustment it was impossible for me to accept that we were no longer able to have a positive interaction in a normal social manner. I knew the fine capabilities inherent in Chester's mind, therefore we did not give up until we absolutely had to. We put up a strong and determined fight. But once I courageously met the realization of these social problems, I was able to focus on the positive potentials in our social life. A short time after Chester stopped playing tennis, his bravery was called upon one more time.

By this time we were living full time in Palm Desert, since we felt the desert air and generally more relaxed environment would be easier for us to handle. Also, nursing and health care was more readily available in a community made up largely of senior citizens.

Giving in to the bliss of ignorance, and not realizing how difficult it would be, he set out to learn to play golf. Though he barely could stand up, I used to take him, daily, to the driving range at our club to hit golf balls. I placed each ball on a tee for him, carefully put the golf club in his hand, pointed him in the right direction, and prayed. Probably due to his previous athletic abilities and his natural rhythm as a musician, almost miraculously he hit the ball. His gallant efforts did not go unnoticed. Soon he had a small group of admirers that watched him. And within this assemblage was an extremely kind gentleman. He became his loyal friend.

One day as we were hitting balls, we were interrupted. "Excuse me, my name is Joe. I've been watching you two every day. How 'bout if I pick up Chester in my golf cart and take him tomorrow," he directed to me "We'll have lunch and play a few holes."

Chester looked up, smiled as if he "were one of the guys," and chimed in, "Sure, I'll be ready whenever you say." And that was the beginning of a devoted and loving friendship. At that moment I thought "the world really is a perfect place."

And in that small corner of the world, there was perfection, as Joe became a very important figure in Chester's life. His own real devotee.

As Chester's illness progressed, even though our socializing became tedious, we actually were invited to a few social gatherings. However, preparing to go to these events was such a lengthy ordeal that by the time we arrived at our destination, Chester's "on" time (the span of time the medications would be effective) had in many instances worn off. He was exhausted and sometimes barely able to walk, let alone converse intelligibly.

The pace was merely too fast for him. Not only was he strained, our friends were ill at ease as well. The best-intentioned of people simply do not know how to act or treat a person who has an illness or is disabled. In fact, I found that most people were even hesitant to question the condition of one who is chronically ill in a simple "How is Chester feeling?" for fear that they might have hurt my feelings rather than showing support to a friend. Many look at a physically challenged person and suddenly are reluctant to speak in normal conversation and quite often they simply shy away, leaving the needy very much in need. Finally, many of our acquaintances were frankly uncomfortable, but for some reason Chester never seemed to notice, or at least didn't let on that he did. I believe that the veil between him and reality was the element that allowed his morale to remain intact. His spirit had been his mightiest weapon, protecting him in the battle against his entire illness. I learned from him that denial, when used properly, can be a positive force in dealing with problems and coping with seemingly impossible challenges. You might say that his denial had been merely a form of optimism and it gave him a positive impetus. In many instances it was quite beneficial for him to go through this part of his life dancing with his eyes closed instead of open to the world and all of its cruelties. Perhaps his naiveté was part of some great master plan that protected him when he said, "I'm not sick, I'm only suffering a temporary setback." He refused to acknowledge the differences between him and the rest of the world, and simultaneously relied only on the similarities that he perceived.

At some point I began to question the quality and depth of the people with whom we socialized. It took a substantial amount of time for me to grasp and face up to what was actually going on in our life, for the indications were ever so subtle. No one really wanted to hurt us, but phone calls that might have begun with "Why don't we get together…", or "What are you guys doing…" just stopped.

An indelible print on my mind was made one evening when I pushed Chester in his wheelchair to the front of the line at a movie. I saw a group of our "casual" friends laughing and joking, having a good time as we passed them.

"You're looking good, Chester. Nice to see you, see ya around." someone said. And then from the background I heard, "Poor guy."

Chester nodded his frail head back at them, and I only hoped that the lump in my throat would not show when I smiled as we hurried past them. I knew we were not wanted anymore. It seemed so final.

Not only were my bruises derived from my husband's hurts and ours as a couple, they also were mine as an individual. I couldn't understand why I wasn't included in our old group now, when before I had been. My heart cried out with hurt and loneliness. But even though I suffered, I never really blamed our friends for not wanting what we had to offer. The situation was frankly just too much for them to handle, and the last thing I wanted was to be pitied, or worse, to be invited somewhere in a condescending manner. Nor did I want to be befriended from obligation by the people around us enjoying life. I said, "No thank you," unless I felt sure that an invitation was genuine and sincere, and was very careful not to subject us to unnecessary humiliation. Thus, I eventually became very selective and began to steer our social life to only very dear friends and family. I chose to socialize only with "the devotees" of life with whom I knew I could trust to love us "no matter what." The main criterion that I sought was of our emotional comfort and safety.

One day as I poured out my heart to a girlfriend, she looked directly at me and said, "Carleen, you can't fight Chester's battles for him. No one will win that way."

Another turning point. I realized that I could not make Chester well and able again. And yet, I had to be big enough to understand and accept the awkward position in which people in general were placed. Without reservation of any kind I had to fully comprehend that my husband and I were the ones afflicted with his Parkinson's disease, and our friends were not. We were in this awful situation together and separate from the rest of the world. Our way through this journey had to be found on our own.

The only problem with this new realization was that I did not know how to live my life as "a married person without a mate," or "a single person with a spouse." From time to time it felt as if there were giant spaces in my existence and I didn't know how to scale those threatening gaps. How far from the conventional lifestyle could I go and still continue to live an acceptable mode of life? As a result of this quandary, I did virtually nothing out of the ordinary for many years. That is, I did nothing, except think, and think, and think. After a time, I started to feel that I was mainly alone. Chester did not mind, because he was content to stay at home and sleep as his illness drained him. Moreover, he still had his caregiver, me, as his constant companion. However, I became enormously lonely and conscious that I had lost my friend, buddy, and dancing partner, and now felt completely alone.

Loneliness in this stage of my life had a strange effect on me. I certainly was not physically alone as I was surrounded by people all the time. Chester was always there, along with his nurses (nursing care had become part of our lives). But oh, how lonely my heart felt, and how extremely empty were my thoughts. I could see Chester as he appeared before me, and even though I actually could communicate with him from time to time, the long intervals in between were too long for my cravings of mind and body. I wanted to have him hear the agonized, quiet scream coming from within my heart. What I would have given for one more argument or confrontation like we had when we were separated years before. Those horrible fights that I hated so much, which touched off our divorce, now would have been heartily welcomed, compared to this deadening silence. How vivid in my mind were the all night talks and discussions we used to have dissecting every corner of our lives, and I even missed our political arguments that went on for days. It was not unusual for the rapport we enjoyed to be envied by our friends; an important issue or thought always was being examined and studied.

Before we were separated, we used to go on long walks with our collie dog every night and debate our philosophies. We strolled securely in the moonlight solving every problem of the world, so we thought. So when that lucid part of our lives vanished, I finally admitted that I could not handle this new pattern of living anymore. I knew then that I needed to interact with another person. I greatly yearned to once more hear another soul react to the world I touched. I had to know that I made a difference in time and space, and needed to know that someone would respond to my being alive, and I to another. In essence, by this time I desperately missed the true spiritual connection with my soul mate.

A milestone occurred for me when we attended our last party together. It was a Christmas celebration in 1991, and twelve Christmases had passed since Chester was first diagnosed with Parkinson's disease. The years of struggling through the illness had taken their toll on his mental and physical condition, and unbeknown to us, the night of the party was just ten days preceding the first of many strokes he was to endure. Though his condition was frail, we were both anxious to join the festivities, and I especially was happy for the invitation to the party.

The party room was magically transformed into a winter wonderland with glittering lights, lovely bright shining ornaments, and colorful decorations wherever you looked. It surely was one of the most beautiful, lavish, and gala events that I had ever attended. The food was sumptuous, the band's music was melodic and romantic. Holiday enchantment gleamed everywhere, and we were once more surrounded by many of our friends. Everyone had a grand and joyous time. That is, almost everyone. Chester sat the whole evening expressionless and hollowed by his illness. He could scarcely walk now without being supported, and I did not know that this beautiful party would be the last social function he would ever attend. It was difficult for him to face such a great social ordeal, and he remained frozen most of the night. At the same time, I watched our friends laugh, joke, and enjoy the exquisite evening as they danced the night away. And how badly I wanted to feel the slats of the dance floor just one time beneath my feet. I imagined myself being twirled around the floor in graceful spins as I enviously glared at the dancers shimmering in their holiday sparkling dresses. I sat motionless, feeling a hurt I could not explain. I felt sad and frustrated as if I were a spectator observing life, but only with the ability to watch. The longer I sat, the more I felt the gaiety surrounding us, and at the same time, the heavier the familiar lump in my throat became. Somehow I knew that it would be the last time we would ever play a part in social moments such as these.

We managed to get through the evening and made our exit just as soon as we could after bidding our forced adieus. As I put on my coat to leave, the tears streamed down my face. I was struck with the truth that the goodbyes that I said were symbolic in that I was also saying goodbye to this social part of my life, as well. I didn't know where I was going in life, I only knew that an important part of my life ended that night. I slowly drove away from the party and started to cry, drowning out the last visions of the gaiety and happiness we left behind. As the music faded into the background of the night I felt Chester reach for my hand on the steering wheel. At first I thought he was reaching for moral support for himself. But he had my pain in the front of his mind.

"It's gonna be all right, honey," he whispered, squeezing my fingers tightly. That's all he could get out. He was so weak.

Trying to control myself, I took a deep breath and whispered, "I know it will, sweetheart."

And then uncontrollably I broke down and cried. In between the deepest sobs I have ever felt, I uttered a few words that would ultimately change my life, *"But I can still dance."*

The next day I talked with one of my friends who was also at the Christmas party. With the hope of finding some answers to the sad and puzzling dilemma through which I was living I openly asked her to help me make some sense of the whole situation. At this time the only thing that I knew was that I felt a monstrous identity crisis and felt as if I didn't know who I was any longer or where I belonged. I also knew that at that point I had hit my emotional bottom.

"What's the real story, my friend? Is there any place at all that I fit in anymore?" I begged for answers, and I got them.

"Car," she said, "we don't want to hurt Chester, so we can't exclude him from our parties and just invite you." She went on after a moment. "Please understand that it's just too hard to include him, too. We just can't."

Not actually walking in their shoes, I did not understand my friends until much later. What I did comprehend at that time, was that I was truly alone. A unique alone. I was not included with Chester, and I was not included without him. I had no hope of an unattached person's "alone" with the prospect of finding a partner, companion, or mate "out there," but I felt a desperately lonely "alone" with thoughts of being permanently placed that way, as we were told it could be another 15 or 20 years that way.

Living through that difficult night and watching the rest of the world enjoy their lives actually turned out to be a fortuitous event for me. This experience enabled me to reach the depth of my feelings and forced me to travel on to the next step in my journey. At that point, I was able to "let go" entirely and be ready to start my climb back up to a place where I could find my own new happiness. For me I needed to be completely ready for a change to take place before it actually could become a reality, and unfortunately, there is no other way to get ready for such a change than to go as far down emotionally as possible.

How strange it was then, that such a small and insignificant incident as being left out of the dance could have set the entire next part of my life in motion. Of course, as I think about my sad feelings that Christmas holiday season, I recognize how dwarfed the importance of my simple life circumstances were in comparison to the horrendous effects of the illness Chester was to experience. Also, I am perfectly cognizant of how minute the problems of my social situation were when simple survival is life's greatest challenge for so many people. And I certainly know well the many crises that develop during the course of a day in caring for a loved one who is ill or disabled. An event as simple as getting dressed or fed can change into a monstrous and frustrating ordeal for both the patient and the caregiver. There were times when I would be in tears from frustration and my heart would be breaking for Chester before I was able to finally get him dressed in a presentable manner.

But knowing that his immaculate style was of the utmost importance to him, we would go through this arduous exercise with the hopes of completing a sometimes seemingly impossible task.

"Please, Chester, try to lift your foot just a little bit higher. I can't get your socks on," I cried one morning as I knelt by his feet. Muffling the sounds of my desperation so no one could hear me, "I can't hold the jacket any longer. Where is your arm? Give it to me."

Each button on his shirt was a major event, and how I hated the winter when heavy sweaters were necessary to fight the cold. It meant one more garment to put on. My heart broke for him every time I had to dress him. The poor dear was so helpless and I felt so terribly hopeless.

And never will I forget the trying events in preparing to go out, just thinking about the difficulties that might lie ahead of us in an evening or simply planning an entrance and exit to our automobile. Many times the logistics of entering a home, office, or restaurant became fearful, gigantic, complicated problems that would have to be solved, to say nothing of the worries that would engulf us at a dinner table.

I also know how frightening and seemingly impossible are the new additional financial burdens added to the caregiver's life. Perhaps at a time and stage when at last an easier life seems feasible, suddenly undeniable responsibilities must be worked out. I went through every one of those traumas in those sixteen years, as every other caregiver most assuredly will. There is no way out. Sacrifices must be endured when one needs to juggle finances for doctors, nurses, medical equipment, and medicine, besides the cost of extra caregivers, if one is even fortunate enough to have a caregiver assistant.

However, just because I was willing to be candid about my circumstances regarding the loss of an accustomed lifestyle, that honesty did not magically transform those problems. Though the problems of a changing social lifestyle may seem to have been "high class problems," they were problems that had to be dealt with, and it felt like one more blow that we didn't need. Until my honesty reached a level that permitted me to seriously address each issue and admit that what I felt after that Christmas party was in the most basic of terms, "entrapment," the problem could not be solved. The sentiment of "where's mine" though selfish as it may have seemed at the time, was the very basis for my being able to acknowledge the pain that I felt. Thus being obliged to accept fully the mixed bag of feelings of being boxed in without knowledge of how to extricate myself from this maze, and at the same time not wanting to, I discovered that I was the source of my own "Catch 22." I was inclined to apologize for my feelings of sadness, thinking they were out of proportion and overreactive. The truth was, even though they were sad feelings, they were mine and had to be recognized for what they were. Loving Chester was not an issue here. I loved him very much, but at that moment the most important thing in the world was that I felt I had no place in a world where "it takes two to tango."

# 5

## The Beat Picks Up

### Freedom

Sad resignation finally left me. I was released from my own self-bondage when I faced squarely my problems and made the decision to no longer be their prisoner. Then, and only then, was I able to begin to enjoy myself and exercise my choices. Whatever guilt was caused by Chester's debilitation diminished to a great degree once I finally began to enjoy the productive and healthy years that I had left. When I began to look beyond Chester's helpless face and body, knowing full well that there was nothing that could be done to make him a healthy person again, I began to feel a new sense of freedom. This is not to say that he was not uppermost in my thoughts. It is unquestionable that if I had the power to return him to good health, I would have stopped at nothing to do so. However, the cold and sad fact was that I could not restore him to a healthy state of being. When I looked at his strong spirit in his tattered and worn body, I saw the high price that he gallantly paid, and the desire to live my own life greatly increased. At the same time I was able to acknowledge that someday I might also be sick and have special needs myself, making the gift of healthy living one to always be greatly cherished.

I learned that one's freedom should not be taken for granted, and we are all vulnerable as long as we live. I used to associate freedom with the privilege of choosing where and how one lives along with the gift of being unshackled. Of course, these are undeniably the most treasured freedoms of all. But one day the definition of freedom changed for me when I sat with Chester in his doctor's office while various neurological tests were being performed.

After what seemed to be quite a long time for Chester's physical and emotional endurance, the doctor kindly said to him, "Chester, you're very brave, as well as being a good patient. I'm sorry that I'm making you so uncomfortable. Bear with me." The doctor did all he could to relieve Chester's physical and mental anguish, but little could be done to stop his trembling.

Ever so quietly Chester answered, "Thanks. It's okay. I'm all right. Please go on." Chester tried so hard to be helpful.

Although the physician acknowledged Chester's agreeable demeanor and apologized for his discomfort, Chester was the one who had to lie there helplessly as the needles from the machine pricked his tender and frail body. As I sat and watched, I noted the difference in our scopes of living. I knew that no matter how brave a patient, or how much goodness Chester possessed, the machine would only give the results of what it was fed. Chester's life was being directed by the piece of complicated equipment in front of us. If I could have changed the electrodes, I would have, but at that moment I knew the real significance of freedom and the exact difference between his imprisonment and my liberties.

After this experience, freedom took on a new meaning for me. I learned that the living within my own body and soul began with a free state of mind. Freedoms attached to liberties such as these were the first ones that had to be treated with respect, for these created my own happiness, and I was likewise responsible for what I ultimately decided to do with the rest of my own life. What remained for Chester was a limited freedom contingent upon another human being. He was dependent on his caregiver for all of his mental and physical needs. His own choices were eliminated as if they were erased and replaced by the unfortunate, inadequate mercy of medical science. The result was that he became a prisoner within his own body. No matter what his inner thoughts were, to a certain extent, his freedom disappeared. The deepest sadness is that his fate could not be changed nor reversed, and his dependency ultimately became exaggerated as his illness advanced.

The tragedy of a chronic illness is increased when the caregiver also relinquishes rights to freedom as well, while still having possibilities for a life to be embellished with quality. Inner peace is spelled *"FREEDOM,"* and since the beginning of time, it has always been worth fighting for. With it, anything is imaginable. Impossible dreams can become realities with freedom, and without it, nothing is possible. Dreams and freedom are interrelated. They produce each other, and are equally the beginning of thoughtful life itself.

During the many unstable years before I acknowledged my freedom, I trudged the narrow road set for me by Chester's illness. Though he never set formal boundaries for the care he needed, he did what is common among chronically ill patients. He controlled both of our lives with his illness by creating the mental and physical atmosphere in which we both lived. Rarely did we compromise on an issue for our mutual satisfaction. Priorities were established according to a one-way train of thought. His way. This kind of life is not unique for a caregiver. Though our lives were neither uncivil nor acrimonious, it was simply a given that our lives were directed primarily by and for Chester and his needs. For years we simply went about our activities, planning and doing whatever was desirable for him. We thought only about what would make his life more comfortable, giving no consideration for anyone else, which coincidentally included me.

Finally, twelve years passed from the inception of the disease, and I realized that this style of living contributed to my depression and repressed sadness. I awakened each morning in a fog-like state and continued the day in a trance. All of my self-identity had diminished, and I moved around in robot fashion, planning each hour of the day around Chester's needs. Unconsciously I created a twenty-four-hour-a-day job for myself with no break in sight. This is not to say that I did not think of what he should have in his life. However, later I also became aware of what I should have in mine, too. Though this long period was grave, the deep depression and saddened spirit that resulted became the catalysts which eventually led me out of the difficult emotional place where I lived.

After great frustration and long suffering with this highly unsatisfactory situation, I decided that many circumstances in our lives had to be negotiable, and we both needed to acknowledge my feelings and needs as well as Chester's. It became apparent that due to Chester's passive control, his illness was devouring my life. The quality of his life was also at the same time reduced by the resentment my deprivation caused me to feel. It was important to redefine where I stood in relation to his illness and remain strong in my decision not to lose myself or my own values when we traveled this new, difficult course that we began.

Once I reached the point of no return and was brave enough to recognize that I was not happy with the way things were, I "came out of the closet" with my feelings. I laid new ground rules and set new boundaries for us that did not hurt either of us anymore. I knew that if I didn't do this, I would be unable to function any longer as a wife, friend, and caregiver. With these gigantic revelations I started to sense new dimensions, and for the first time felt a sense of renewed hope.

As I reached toward the unknown to satisfy the yearnings of my own spirit, the beat and rhythm of my life picked up. Though the wounds were plentiful, so were the scars of their healing. And thus it happened that eventually I regained some innate rights that restored my independence. At last I heard the bell of freedom ringing in my ears, resonating in my soul. And then I understood what the ancient Roman slave, Epictetus, meant when he declared, "No man is free who is not master of himself."

When I realized that I could not please everyone all of the time, and finally discovered that I was in line for some attention and strokes too, I became able not only to clarify some of my own short-term goals, but also to mobilize the process of obtaining them as well. As a result of this reversal of attitude and finding a new posture by which to live, Chester became a natural benefactor. The resentments that I once felt for his illness were replaced by a new degree of patience and a deeper devotion to love him.

For a long time I worried about Chester's future, our future, and my future, as well. Although I rarely mentioned my panic, thinking of the days ahead, I worried constantly about the severe alterations in our lives that Chester's illness would require. I imagined how it would be to have the responsibility of his nurse, his wheelchair, and a hospital bed in our home, and thought endlessly of the terror that would engulf us while living with an advanced Parkinson's disease patient.

How frightened I was when I went shopping for medical supplies after his first stroke. The clerk in the store gathered together the items on my shopping list that I was directed to buy by the hospital nurse. Then in a kindly manner the clerk pointed to a store display of a trapeze contraption hanging above a bed. "Do you need one of those?"

"No! Just give me what's here!" I shrieked. "It just couldn't be," I thought. All I could think of was running away. I was horrified by the unfamiliarity of it all, overwhelmed with terror—the nurse, the equipment, and as always, his illness. But mainly, uncontrollable fear!

We had basked in the luxuries of a fashionable lifestyle in the past, and frankly I was terrified to think that Chester's illness could progress to the point when he might need a trapeze apparatus to assist him out of bed. Or even worse, that he might never leave his bed at all. Though I ached over the debilitation of his body and spirit, I could not accept the visualization of him with the walker and wheelchair that I purchased that day. At that moment in time I could not suddenly step into that frame of reference.

Oddly enough, that part of our lives gradually fell into place with much less trauma than I had imagined. Each stage occurred slowly, and once we reached a new level of the illness, it proved much less frightening than the road to it appeared. The parts that gave me intense trepidation were the fearful thoughts of exaggerated fantasies I harbored. But once I was able to reverse this negative process and turn the fears into hopes for myself, I was able to rebalance my emotions and live within a quieter, more gentle state of mind. As a result, we bravely faced each new episode and development as it happened, and eventually I found my life being restored and it finally began to work again.

One by one, the pages of the calendar had turned. Days had turned into weeks, months, and yes, years, until finally I gained a welcomed new perspective. Fortunately, with my health still very much intact I began to enjoy each carefully planned day with a deeper respect for myself as well as my husband. Once more I walked down the street with my old bounce to a happy gait and knew I was walking in the direction I wanted to go. I sensed that the scent of flowers and rays of sunshine were mine to enjoy. But more than that, I saw beyond the sunset a glimmer of hope waiting for me, and with new optimistic affirmations in my mind, it was difficult for depression and fear to creep in. I chose to do only that which produced the utmost joy for me, which at the same time would not interfere with Chester's care. The primary goal here was not to waste nor lose one precious minute, and I realized how lucky I was to have had a second chance in life while I was still physically and psychologically healthy. I became aware whenever I was in the midst of joy, and conscious when in a happy state of mind. Once you lose something, its value seems to increase if you are fortunate enough to find it again. I realized this, and thus I became conscious of the ability to enjoy reality when reality was enjoyable.

Through those difficult years I learned to live with a great deal of sadness, but I also learned the difference between that level and a higher plane of happiness. If there was a place for me in a happy emotional atmosphere, then you can be sure, I was there. No joy passed before me without my taking full part in it. Most of all, I was aware that I was given the greatest gift of all, the chance to be healed from my part of Chester's illness. When one person in the family has a chronic affliction, it naturally becomes a family illness, and everyone involved is affected. The wise credo of The Well Spouse Foundation relates that, "When one is sick, two need help."

Even though in some ways I felt that I lost a portion of my life, I know how fortunate I was to have been able to continue my life, and in a multitude of ways attained even greater insights into the meaning of my existence. This new way of living taught me the difference between what was valuable and what was not. In addition these thoughts gave me the option to feel important and of value to myself as well as to the person I cared for. Not only could I, and did I exist, I enjoyed my own life, as well.

Even though I greatly feared my unusual life style, it proved to be not only fun and exciting, but it also offered me the opportunity to change my goals. Instead of taking tedious, conventional routes, I ventured on less traditional paths. Instead of seeking "the pot of gold at the end of the rainbow," I realized that the rich rewards of life are sprinkled along the way of the journey. I was given the gift of time to take risks and chances, fully understanding that there was no immediate reconciliation of my gains or losses. Being my own judge and jury, I reaped the results of my efforts. I learned that it was no sin to fail, the only crime was not to try.

One may wonder how the constricted life of a caregiver could actually be free. Once more the complexity of the problem was far more massive than the simple solution. As so many of life's questions are answered in the simplest terms, so were mine.

First and foremost, I looked directly in front of me and watched and listened intently for every possible opportunity. I made deep spiritual and intimate friendships with people that I might never have chosen to be with had Chester and I continued our casual business and social acquaintances. The only thing with which I was concerned in finding companions and friends, was the character of those with whom I was relating and what real value could be exchanged in our lives. It became interesting to venture away from the usual mentality with which I was accustomed for so many years. Though the traditional personality certainly had its proper place in my life, so did the unusual, if the quality of the individual with whom I spent time was stimulating and meaningful to me. It was fun to pick and choose my new friends, carefully measuring their valuable intrinsic qualities. As a result I was gifted with worthy and precious associations with companions I greatly admired and I developed worthwhile friendships that I shall always treasure.

Neither was time a factor anymore, since I was aware that only the present was at stake. Not the future, and certainly not the past. No clock ticked in the background of my life. I had all the time in the world to explore new horizons as long as none of the beats of these measures were wasted. The hours of time seemed to have wings as I watched them fly by, and they reached their highest degree of value only when they were gone. Time continued no matter what I did, so I found that the trick was to feel the rhythm being sure that all the while I was entirely honest about my needs, never minimizing my freedom for even a minute. Nonsense, time wasters, or "fillers" had no place in my world anymore. Those were the only things for which I had no time. The knots that bound me to false, unimportant old ideas and values were untied. I broke patterns with meaningless restrictions, and replaced them with the substance of my own true needs.

Basically, I did what I wanted to give myself pleasure, making sure not ever to hurt nor endanger Chester in any way. Although I always had his welfare at heart, closely alongside was my own. I valued my own good life, enjoyed the newly found self-esteem to which it was attached, and realized the need to continually feed that self-worth in practical ways.

There were many routes from this new place in my heart, and I chose to travel the one leading me "out there" in society for my own therapy. This philosophy worked for me and kept me going the last years of this dreadful family illness. The smile on my face and in my heart was the result of the desires and hopes that set my freedom in motion in the first place. This in no way minimized the importance of therapy and support groups, because they certainly were essential at some point to me, as a caregiver. Though they did play an important part in my life, rather than sitting around a table and talking about problems with those having the same ills, I mainly chose to experience the solutions to the painful issues by feeling free to go out and act, do, feel, run, leap, move, think, enjoy, and yes, to DANCE.

# 6

## This is My Dance

### Fighting Guilt and Depression

As the earth tilts on its axis bringing sunshine to the days of summer, so did my own world pivot from the winter of my depression to the first glimpse of springtime's hope. The tired look I had worn for so long did not fit my inner being anymore, nor was I comfortable with the strain and worry that had lurked deeply within me in the past. No longer did I see a sad person as I gazed in my mirror that noteworthy spring day. My senses were alive now, as I watched the rays of sunshine surround the image of my own reflection. Staring straight ahead at myself in the mirror, I spoke aloud to the reflection in front of me, as if I were discussing my problems and seeking answers from a friend. I questioned the crucial issue of my journey in life and my right and reason to live.

"I've come so far now," I said to this imaginary companion. "There must be a place for me in this world. A place where I can feel the sun warming my own heart with happiness again."

My eyes penetrated my soul, and as my heart swelled with hope, I went on to my visionary confidant. "Someday I'll smile at the moon, and not fear the dark of night. I know the sun will shine for me tomorrow. Fear will be replaced by a new confidence and I will be free."

A moment of truth then grabbed me, and I was sure that I would soon be enjoying the promises of life that I instinctively knew were waiting for me.

Until this time, I had continually blamed Chester's illness for my sick feelings. His difficulties had conveniently provided the excuses I needed to set aside my personal desires, and ironically, they offered a bizarre protection as a retreat from positive actions on my own behalf. It had been easier to complain of my own poor health and careworn state rather than facing up to what I needed to do to improve myself. But at this turning point in my survival, I looked toward a positive existence built around happiness. I realized that I could blame Chester's maladies on his disease, but that it was necessary for me to take responsibility for the direction of my own life. I knew that if I stayed masked any longer and refused to recognize my own relationship to his illness, I probably would spend the rest of my life with an imprisoned soul, unnecessarily tending personal ailments and deficiencies which were not actually mine.

Without hearing a spoken response, I received answers from my inner self that early spring day in 1992, and I came upon the first of many solutions which proved to be the bend in the road that would eventually lead me back to healthy living again.

To this point I had been proud of being an adept and devoted caregiver, and if there had been an award for *"Over-Caregiver of the Year,"* I would certainly have won first prize. I had been overzealous in giving physical and emotional support to make Chester as happy and comfortable as possible, taking little thought to my own needs. Excessive gallantry for Chester's protection forced me to carry this devotion and care beyond my own safety. As a result, as it so commonly is in a caregiver's plight, my husband's chronic affliction became my illness. All aspects of my life became affected, including my professional, financial, and social life, along with my mental health and stability, and my own physical condition. Then I knew it was crucial that I practice self-healing on the person with the hopeful eyes that I saw in the mirror that sunny spring day.

It wasn't important to distinguish if my flight from life outside the confines of Chester's world had been heroic behavior, or if my withdrawal merely disguised a kind of cowardice which protected me from facing my own real world. Nonetheless, it happened. At long last it became clear I had to heal myself, first and foremost. I realized that being sick didn't work for me any longer, and I understood fully that I held my own life in my own hands.

It was as if I had just been given an innocent baby to care for, and I had to thoughtfully protect her. I realized that I needed to give myself tenderness, respect, and love with the hope that I could regain my ability to make positive decisions leading to a healthier and more normal life. Of course I recognized that this fantasy was only a dream. But illusions are powerful tools, and soon they were replaced with realistic images and real life choices.

Once these revelations occurred there was a dynamic clarity in my purpose, and it became easier to make changes rather than remaining the sick person I had been. When I became entirely ready to stop existing within the circle of problems that faced me, even though they were undeniably real problems, I was able to see alternatives to my life that before had been unavailable. It was then possible for me to choose how to live my life based on my own free will. With this idea in mind, I decided to give "living" a try.

I recognized that real problems do not necessarily mean, nor must result in, defeat nor sadness. In fact, perplexing as they were, many of them became catalysts for finding solutions. With honest feelings I candidly appraised my life. Initially I spent a lot of time assessing the entire picture while carefully listening and watching for cues for each pending step. I refused to accept any form of insincerity and demanded from myself a strict and rigid standard of not being satisfied with less than what I rightly deserved. When fear rumbled within, I tried to remember the hopeful eyes that I had seen in the mirror, or the infant baby I imaginarily cradled in my arms. These two images were strong enough to keep me focused on a new and positive direction. In essence, they gave me the strength that introduced me to my real self. These fictitious, symbolic images ironically reversed my sick reality and offered me the opportunity to take responsibility for my own life and actions. More than anything, these imaginary thoughts opened my eyes to an important command to simply "grow up" and face a part of life from which I wanted to run.

As time went on, the difficulty or intensity of the problem to solve did not matter. Although the issues became more serious, the solutions became more obvious because the exercise was unpolluted by biased thoughts. Constructive measures were the goal and finding new methods of obtaining a happy life became exciting. Coping with troublesome situations, making important decisions, and finally living life within a comfortable rhythm was a process with which I eventually became accustomed. As in any other skill that I ever learned, I repeated the lesson until the memory was ingrained in my mental muscles.

I liken the experience to learning to dance. When you first go on the dance floor you feel awkward and unbalanced. Then, as you repeat the steps, you suddenly learn where to put your feet. After stepping on a few toes, the rhythm starts to feel natural, you suddenly develop a new grace, and before you know it, you're dancing!

The hardest part was to unlearn old destructive ideas and habits which were familiar. Old habits die hard. It took a lot of serious work on my part to even begin this new way of thinking. Long-time, ingrained muscle memory had to be changed. Though I didn't completely understand what was happening, I knew that my old way of life was not comfortable anymore. Moreover, I didn't intend to give up the life I hoped for until I made a sincere effort to change what I thought was blocking me.

Completely entrenched in a fight for my own survival, I held onto the hope and dream that I would be able to find out how to retrieve my own healthy life again. I had to learn how to give care to another human being with whom I was united and still hold onto the core of my own identity. Occasionally, I slipped back into my old feelings of sadness and depression, but I found that I didn't have to surrender entirely to each temporary slip.

Change can be a scary process. It requires releasing various patterns that may have been part of one's entire lifetime. It also can be an agonizingly slow act of peeling one layer back a tiny bit at a time. Qualities were revealed to me which before lay hidden within my soul. Never tapped before, they were at last available when I discovered that I had enough will to change and enough desire to move in a direction that I finally felt was forward.

As I continued my quest to find some happiness and pleasure in this new and changing role, I became aware of various new and subtle insights that became useful in reforming my life. I began to take some risks and found that there was more life out there than I ever dared to imagine. It was all mine for the taking. I simply had to remove the harness of self-imposed restraints and enjoy the life that was there awaiting me. As others have observed, freedom cannot always be granted. Sometimes it must be taken.

In order to cross that unfamiliar threshold of life, I grasped at each opportunity as it appeared, and in my venture doors opened where I found a new kind of courage. It became clear that without taking chances in an intimidating world, without boldly standing up to unfamiliar danger in the line of emotional fire, without bravely facing possible hurt by rejection, there would be no gain and certainly no change in my life. I needed to feel as if I was afraid of nothing. I needed to conceal the most obvious as well as my most private inhibitions, and of course, the greatest difficulty of all was to withhold the knowledge of these fears even from my own self.

Relying on this new-found bravery, I actually began to live a desirable life while still being a caregiver to a chronically ill and, often, helpless person. I was objective in this highly subjective relationship and recognized myself as a whole person. Even though I was involved in this sorrowful situation, the demand for answers finally took precedence over the acceptance of seemingly insoluble questions. For the first time in my life I considered myself on the offense on the line of scrimmage rather than on the defense—and what a great time for the upset of the game! At last I knew what it meant to enjoy the delicious taste of victory.

Respecting my new way of thinking, I responded to life with a graceful finesse. I possessed a goal, a promise to myself. And when I fell short of what I was seeking I didn't completely give in to an immediate defeat. If I felt insecure, I took a deep breath and recalled my fantasy images. I closed my eyes and imagined hearing a baby's contented murmurs, or visualized my own happy face smiling back at me in the mirror. Just a little positive imagination gave the boost of energy which returned me to a steady course.

Shortly after my encounter with this new courage, I detected that it had laid the foundation for another valuable asset. I discovered the power of choice. No longer did I have anxiety over decisions made in my behalf. I set fears aside, simply looked at the alternatives, and began to take chances when choices were needed. It became a game for me, and fun, since most of the points were not crucial, and now I was actually a participant in the event. Carefully scrutinizing the benefits and possible results of the situation, I considered the possible negative aspects for Chester versus the plausible positive aspects for myself, rather than automatically giving way to all of his desires as I had done in the past. Previously I'd had difficulty trying always to come up with the right decision. Now, I didn't lose sight of the new issue that had revealed itself, which of course was my own physical and mental health. Often there was neither a right nor wrong answer, but simply an answer which considered both our needs.

Making choices was therefore another fresh thought process and a vehicle which brought me a little closer to emotional freedom. After some practice, my style of choice became a graceful art. The more I practiced and the more creative I got, the easier it became.

This miraculous new way of assessing my life gave me the strength to look beyond my living room, TV, and bedroom, where previously I had only my lap shawl to give me warmth and security. At the same time, and of the greatest importance, this new view offered hope that there truly was a life for me beyond my husband's bed, wheelchair, and nurse. I had the strength to take baby steps "out there" when it would have been easier and safer to remain within my cloistered, self-imposed incarceration. Setting aside the familiar became easier as my new skills improved, until finally the difficult life I was leading was no longer acceptable to me simply because it was what I was used to. I was able to peek through my living room curtains and see the world enjoying happiness, a part to which I knew I belonged.

For the first time in a long time I started to care about myself, beginning with the way I looked. My physical appearance became of the utmost importance. I stopped wearing sloppy blue jeans, sweats, and sneakers, and told myself that I always had to be "squeaky clean" and look as perfect as possible. My hair had to be neat and done nicely, and the final product had to be military perfect. There was a definite improvement in how I looked when I changed my course of action and started to clean up my act during this "raise my morale" period. Instead of seeing pitiful eyes staring back at me when I looked in the mirror, I saw the face of a friend, telling me that I could not go out unless I passed a critical inspection. Though this stress on physical appearance may seem senseless and unimportant, the improvements I made reflected on my "insides" at the same time. I felt that I had to start with the basics. I promised myself that I wouldn't leave home without every tool I had that helped me get rid of the lump in my throat and stop my endless tears. It seemed as if I had spent the whole previous year weeping, and my distraught feelings prevented me from experiencing any pleasant reality that came my way.

They say living a good life is primarily an "inside job." No way! For me I had to build on what I could see first. And soon nobody knew how sad and scared I was because I looked fine. Then one day I started to actually feel like I looked, and I walk like I talked.

Towards the beginning of this new re-enlightenment of my life, one afternoon Chester and his nurse were waiting for me to take them to the doctor. Before, I had always been ready for them whenever I was needed. This time, however, there was a major difference. I was not.

Chester waited in his wheelchair with his nurse, Maria, by his side. "What's the matter, Carleen, why aren't you ready? What are you doing?" Chester asked.

"Don't you feel well? Why are you so nervous?" Maria chimed in. "What are you looking for?" she continued, as I opened and closed every drawer in my bedroom.

"We're late, we have to go," Maria insisted.

With new assertiveness, I declared, "I'm not ready."

A revelation happened that day. I knew something was different when I wouldn't leave home until I could find just the right earrings to wear. I couldn't go out unless I matched. Somehow I didn't feel completely dressed unless I was checked out entirely and passed inspection by the new "me." This may seem like a small thing, but it was the beginning of a pride in myself that had been reborn. And as in any other birth, though the experience was painful, the joy that followed was likewise satisfying and rewarding.

These bits and pieces of the redefinition of my life became fun for me, and actually I began to enjoy each approaching challenge. When I eventually reached the other side of my inner self and felt an inward change, I began to rebuild, inside and outside. I developed the greatest courage of all when I started to feel changes in my attitude, and I knew things were really different when I began saying "Fine, thank you, never better, how are you?" and actually meant it. I became so proficient at "acting as if I were okay" that one day I didn't need to act anymore.

A great test of my courage then occurred when I consciously began to rank some of my needs ahead of Chester's desires. I had to be candid enough to admit the weakness in the well-known message that, "If I took care of myself then I would be a better and happier caregiver, and better for my husband as well." This is good sentiment, and sounded fine and noble. However, the truth was that though Chester benefited from my caregiving when I was happy, when I took care of myself and answered my own needs, then ultimately, I was a happier person too. Chester undoubtedly benefited from the side effects of this process, but the goal became to acknowledge and respect my desires for the betterment of my own life as well. Recognizing that I deserved some preference and attention became an important factor in my existence and a necessary process for me to finally endorse.

This, of course, produced some (pardon the overused expression) "guilt." Guilt feelings were the ones with which I needed help the most, since without unlocking this terrible and troublesome barrier I knew I would always remain a prisoner within my own soul. The feelings that guilt produced were the inhibitors and enemy of everything positive that I had worked so hard to achieve. Unfortunately, guilt grabbed me with octopus-like tentacles and squeezed me tightly until my breath was gone. Its arms had to be unwound from my conscience and I was set free from its unshakable grasp only when I had the guts to stand up to it and entirely let go. I finally identified it as the strange and powerfully illusive element that it was.

In a paradoxical way, a negative can sometimes produce a positive; however, the negativity that guilt introduced only reproduced its own ugly self, guilt. Guilt was simply a waste of time and served no useful purpose, benefited no one, and was never an instigator for any forward steps that I took. This is not to say that it didn't need attention. Of course it did, because addressing it was very important to my progress. I liken guilt to having a headache in that it will go away faster if you take an aspirin, and it is likely to persist an indefinite time unless you take action to remove it. Unfortunately, there isn't a pill for guilt, but I found that the best antidote for it was simply to keep on trudging.

I needed to be aware that I was walking through guilt-filled moments which were only feelings. They were not reality unless I made them so. Whenever I bravely faced this enemy, my strength increased commensurate with the amount of guilt that I removed. I counseled myself, "Get rid of this malady as soon as you can, and waste as little time on this emotion as possible. Don't deny yourself one extra minute of happy feelings that are borne from life's truth with which your enemy, guilt, is interfering."

Oddly, once guilt and its brother, depression, became only memories, I found vast, empty voids in my mind and heart that needed to be filled. New segments of time became available, and I needed to open up vistas of fresh ways in which I might live. It's amazing how much time guilt can waste.

Closing the door on any addiction is basically the same, whether it be alcohol, drugs, nicotine, relationships, or guilt. Once you replace the old habit with a new and pleasurable one, then, and only then can and will the addiction be eliminated. My desire to seek the worthwhile friendships on my own eventually became the positive factor that I needed, replacing my feelings of any remaining guilt. When I stopped pondering the feelings of useless guilt, the thoughts of venturing out into a happier existence became less intimidating.

All at once I ceased worrying about what Chester's reactions might be to my temporary absences, and without guilt or fear of reprisal, I sought new company and companionship. Here again, a new test of courage was laid out before me. I faced the issue straight on, and acted fearlessly as I listened to the music in my heart. Not surprising, once more when my motives were honest and direct, without manipulation of any kind, the results were favorable. I simply acted as an adult enjoying well-deserved and long overdue friendships in a proud and happy manner. When I had the courage to face this delicate issue without guilt, I managed to bring back to my relationship with my husband one hundred percent of me for us to enjoy together.

This new breakthrough of finding companionships of and on my own became an important solution to the loneliness that I felt for so long. As a result, once more my husband became the indirect recipient of my new, pleasurable experiences. After I spent some time away from my responsibilities, I always returned home refreshed with a genuine desire to enjoy Chester more. I believe it is the same in all relationships, that it is absolutely vital each person bring all of his potential to the association with one another in order for theirs to be a complete and joyful union. One person can't rely on his mate to fill in his own gaps, while only bringing bits and pieces of his being to the relationship, and still expect a solid feeling to ensue. Therefore, as I cultivated my own social life and rebuilt my own self-worth, I found that I truly brought a happier me not only to my husband, but to whomever I touched.

Practically speaking, this is where my personal support groups came in. My friends and family were loving, loyal, and honest. The same people who had spoken to me frankly about Chester after the crucial Christmas party the year before came forth with ever-memorable, sincere support for me at this time. They urged me to go out, make new friends, get my own life started, and "lighten up." Probably the toughest love that I received is what caused me to be able to take the giant steps towards my own recovery and reach a measure of happiness and freedom. These dear friends seemed to have had a sixth sense for me while being aware of when to love me gently and when to encourage me to stand upright on my own. They became one more valuable link in the chain of solutions that allowed me to solve the problems that I faced. Therefore, as a result of their scrupulous integrity and limitless devotion, I was fortunate to have developed an attitude of *joie de vivre* that sustained me through many tough times.

By far the most dynamic and courageous solution emerged from a discovery in the purest form of morality. Finally, no alternatives were left for me but to move ahead in the quest for my own life. With the deepest honesty, sincerity, and loyalty, and with my heart filled with compassion,

I stared into the eyes of the man whom I deeply loved, and spoke to him. I reached out my hands to him, and before I could say a word, the moisture of his palms told me that he knew what I was going to say.

"Chester, my darling, I have to ask for your help. I've always counted on your strength and support," I said. Looking for a sign, I paused, and then went on, "We've been together for 27 years, and one more time I need your help. We've loved each other through times good and bad, and have made it through impossible odds. We've had the guts to fight the world together, and now we've got to have the guts to go one more round."

He didn't say a word. He just looked at me. My God, what was he thinking? I prayed I didn't hurt him. He had suffered enough. But I knew that I had to take that risk.

I reached down in my soul as far as I could to the deepest point of faith that I had. I took a deep breath. "Chester, what shall I do? What can we do? I'm still healthy, and only six years younger than you were when you first found out that you had Parkinson's disease (I was 54 at that time, and he was 60 at the time of his diagnosis). What if I have only these few years left to live a normal life. I'm scared, sweetheart, but I need to live too. Please, please help me."

We were quiet for several minutes. The only sounds were our hearts beating. He listened to mine—I heard his. Both our eyes filled with tears.

Chester never messed around. In his direct and to the point way of dealing with life, he made it sound so simple.

"Don't miss anything in life, Carleen. Go out and have some fun." He made a gesture with his hand to say he meant it, then continued, "Do it all, It's okay. I'm behind you." His face was once more relaxed. In a peculiar way I believe he was relieved because he knew we had to go in that direction and he felt that he made the decision.

I felt as if I could almost see his soul blessing me that day. In those few short minutes he performed the most generous and valiant act of love that was humanly possible. I knew, without a doubt, that Chester would support me through our lifetime together, and that we really were ending this part of our lives on the same side, as a team. In a sense, we had become caregivers for each other.

After so many years, my mourning period had ended, and we were able to continue dancing to whatever music life played for us. Instinctively, I knew the greatest steps were ahead for me, and that it would be necessary for me to continue my own bravery, as Chester had done throughout his illness. I learned much from Chester through the years, but I'm sure the greatest lesson of all he taught me was that I could be bold enough to say "yes" to life when it was easier to say, "I can't."

# ７

# *The Music Gets Louder*

## *Practicing Viable Solutions*

Distress. Frustration. Anxiety. "Help!" I cried from within. "Borrow, or steal if you have to, but get help right away," to myself once more I continued. "Help is the only thing that will lead me out of this dilemma," I wailed.

From the depths of my own anguish I knew that I had to have some time to call my own. For me. Every caregiver needs relief from responsibilities for a period of time, so they can separate themselves from the illness. I did, too. Even though I wasn't quite sure how to accomplish it, I was confidant that my sanity would be returned only when I either sought assistance from relatives and friends, or hired professional help. It became all too clear that I was involved with a family illness, and I was not the only member of the family. The entire responsibility didn't have to be mine even though it seemed as if the rest of the world might have preferred it to be that way. Chester had grown children and relatives who were perfectly capable of offering some assistance. The time had finally come for everybody to take part.

I told myself I had to start there, even though I knew that Chester's family would not be the final answer. I worried about being a burden to anyone, but I knew that this was not the time for pride. Someone else had to give me the periods of relief that I desperately needed, or surely I would have gone out of my mind. Help was not a luxury. Not only was help necessary in crisis periods, these breaks had to become part of my routine if I were to survive anytime at all, let alone to endure the many years ahead that the doctor had promised me. To enjoy some kind of rewarding lifestyle while "I could still dance," I realized that help was an indispensable requisite for my life. Moreover, help was the binding that held together all who were involved. As a group effort the task was much easier than one person trying to do it all alone.

Though everyone close to the situation was aware of their basic responsibilities, I was careful not to let the family and friends I went to for assistance feel as if I were dumping my responsibility onto them, but rather they were merely helping me with mine. Primarily, it was mine. But they were involved too—they had to be. However, once I openly asked these loved ones to recognize their part in this family crisis, I found that they actually were happy to give whatever assistance they could. They, in fact, became a nurturing, soothing balm for Chester, and me. I certainly benefited from the free time, and Chester enjoyed the additional attention of friends and family members in his life.

The key for me was to reach out for my own survival. No one handed it to me. Perhaps in past decades or generations, and maybe even in smaller, more rural communities, one could count on society at large to step forward and help a friend in a time of crisis. Nowadays, and especially in large cities, more and more people are self-obsessed and concerned mainly with their own welfare. Life seems to move along so rapidly with everyone having so little extra time. Unless assistance is specifically solicited, people seem to wear blinders and can only see their own immediate needs. Family groups are often the same. In fact, the help I received from my husband's family was limited, as their lives were also complicated as everyone's seemed to be. However, when I specifically requested aid, they were there for us. I truly understood their predicaments, at the same time trying not to resent the fact that I was most involved and they were not. It's as if we are all given a basket of things in our lives. We open our basket, and we find good and bad, happy and sad, strong and frail, healthy and diseased. Though it's normal to wish for everything to be good all the time, we live according to what we have been given, and there's no way to return the items that we don't like.

The most loyal and loving attention Chester received was from his dear friend, Bob. With genuine affection, Bob cheered his life, visiting him several times a week all through the long illness, never appearing to be burdened by the stays. Though it was not often necessary to request his assistance for the sake of relieving me, I appreciated knowing he was there brightening Chester's life with his eager visits and regular phone calls.

I loved watching Chester's face light up when the phone rang and Chester heard Bob on the other end of the line say, "Just called to see how you're doing, buddy. Want some company today?"

Chester looked at me with a broad, happy smile and said casually, "Bob's on his way over. Don't make lunch for me, he's bringing something special."

And when the visit ended, I noticed the genuine pleasure on Bob's face when he left our home. In general, I found that people were happy to help when they knew what they did was an appreciated endeavor. Chester's family also seemed to feel satisfaction when they left his side after a caregiving visit, as a positive involvement with someone that they loved was experienced.

My life changed instantly with this new way of evaluating things. I relaxed for the first time in a very long time, and I started to crave a freedom that I had almost forgotten existed. I long had dreamt of such a change, and as the fantasy and passion for freedom increased, the obstacles that appeared to be in my way were removed one by one.

When the phone rang, I then had hopes that it would be for me. "Can you play golf with the girls and have lunch?" I imagined a voice at the other end of the line saying. Or perhaps, "How about going to a movie, a lecture, play bridge, or *dance?*"

"I mustn't get carried away," I thought. "But oh, wouldn't it be nice. Someday, some way, somehow," I whispered under my breath.

And once I reached this level of thinking the process fell into place for me. All at once it became absolutely necessary to prudently prioritize all of our needs—mine and Chester's. I knew that each step was a crucial one, for the outcome would determine how I would live the rest of my own life and how much quality it would have.

Even though family and friends were helpful, I knew I would never get enough assistance from them to completely rectify the situation. I evaluated the situation carefully and only after a great deal of deliberation was able to decide that indeed we were ready for a live-in caregiver. I knew the gains would be beneficial, but the question was also about sharing my home and my husband with another person. Though this one particular decision laid the groundwork for so many opportunities that followed and opened doors to miraculous emotional resolutions for me, getting to the solution and solving each part of the problem was still burdensome. I had to look at the total picture from the whole perspective, judging the entire package rather than the various parts of the situation individually before I could finally move ahead.

First and foremost, the additional financial expense for a live-in helper seemed awesome. Care assistants cost a lot of money that I was not used to spending. I had to decide that I was willing to forego certain enjoyments of my life and reevaluate my wants, needs, and desires, subordinating some of them to this important issue at hand. I had to mentally move certain activities from the classification of necessities in my mind to a much lower rank of dispensable pleasures. My reordered life meant giving up parts of cherished routines and otherwise altering my lifestyle. In effect, the decision asked me to admit that I was ready to move on to the next big change in our lives and move on just a little faster than I may have wanted.

Hiring outside help was one of the most difficult choices I had to make during this long period of illness. However, in some ways the decision was also the easiest to make because this one was based not only on Chester's needs, but for the first time would ultimately result in my benefit as well. And what I gave up amounted to virtually nothing compared to the revitalization of a free mind that I received through the assistance of my live-in careperson.

Clearly, the most crucial factor in my emotional balance was that I finally did seek this needed help. However, it was twelve long years into Chester's illness before I finally acted to remedy the situation. By that time Chester was in the advanced stages of Parkinson's disease, and he was greatly dependent on someone else to assist him with many of his basic needs.

It was painful to watch a once powerful and strong man lie still, waiting to be helped into and out of bed, being assisted in tasks that healthy people take for granted. It was pathetic to know that he couldn't get dressed by himself or put on his own shoes and socks, and it was terribly sad to stand close by when he showered and used the bathroom for fear that he might fall. There were many years that he could not independently go to the kitchen sink for a glass of water, and using the telephone or TV remote-control became a major chore and achievement, and ultimately an impossibility. All of those things are serious, but surely the most painful words I ever heard were, "Help me, I can't get up."

Eventually I had to realize that it was similarly very difficult and sad for me to stand by him guarding his movements all day long and then to continue this vigil all through the night. Several times during the night I had to lift this 170 pound man back and forth, into and out of bed for bathroom trips. Many of my nights were totally sleepless. As a result of this schedule I was quite often brought to tears from my own physical and mental exhaustion. The intense care he required during the day, the difficult nocturnal schedule, plus the added responsibilities of business that I had to handle caused me to feel strained and pressured, and most of the time plainly overworked and overstressed. Through the years it had taken its toll.

Unfortunately, I waited until I was somewhat debilitated myself before I finally hired live-in help. When I did go down this path, however, I felt as if I had been suddenly released from the chains that had held me down. The lump in my throat slowly went away, and I began to take deep breaths not fearing that each one would be my last. One day I realized that there was no need to cry anymore.

Though I still felt sad and deeply sorry for my husband, at least I was able to see a little light at the end of the tunnel for our overall living situation. I slowly began to perceive the building of blocks of my own emotional stability, and my physical health began the process of rejuvenation. I then dared to think beyond the past, to see part of my own life being returned to me in the present, and, tentatively at first, to actually visualize a future. At last, and after so many years, when I looked in my mirror I saw myself as an individual human being and not the shadow of what I thought was.

Definitely, the hardest part of finding a caregiver was to take the first step. But when I did, I entered the first phase of my climb upwards from the slough of despair to where once again I could see the sunlight. However, help is like any other medication—it can cure one problem, but there may be side effects from the remedy. There is no doubt that help in the house brought me the freedom and physical relief that I needed for the cure of my part of the illness, but a new set of demands and stresses developed. For one, I had to endure frustrating moments teaching the new caregiver to take charge of various parts of our regular routine and life.

We took for granted many daily tasks because we lived with them on a regular basis. Then when I tried to teach someone else the important measures of our schedule of nutrition, medication, and general way of living, the gift of their time perhaps seemed like merely one more burden to handle. My patience was tested when someone new just entered the routine of our life. Even though the intrusion was invited, there was still a feeling of invasion at the initial stages of turning a portion of our lives over to a stranger. Besides coping with a new personality, it was necessary to adjust to the mere fact that someone strange was living in my house, and more particularly, another woman was sleeping in the master bedroom with my husband!

However, no matter how long the list of excuses was, and I had compiled a lengthy one, for me a live-in assistant was the only solution. I said that there wasn't room in our home for such an arrangement. Then, I made room. I had to give up living in our bedroom, moved into the small guest room, and compromised on my own sleeping conditions, telling myself that I would benefit in the long run. And indeed I did.

Soon after this great change was made, I had to deal with Chester's reluctance to release me from his constant disposal. He, of course, only wanted me to take care of him as he felt safe and comfortable with the existing arrangement. Even though he was used to me, I knew that I had to make him perceive the situation.

I sat down next to him, and said gently, but assertively, "Chester, there's no alternative. We'll both benefit from extra help, and you've got to compromise one more time."

Deep inside I felt awful asking him to give up anything else when I was well aware how much had already been removed from his life. But I knew there was no other way. I could not go on being glued to him every minute anymore, and I also knew that he'd have to understand. I saw no other way than to be honest with him and hoped he would hear me.

"You have to be willing to try this out, so maybe, hopefully we can regain some control in our lives again. It will be better for both of us." I would not relent. I was aware that this would be one of the most important talks that we would have, and he needed to agree with me or it wouldn't work.

In his soft-spoken manner, he simply said, "Okay, I'll try." I took a deep breath and relaxed for the moment.

It's strange that sometimes, when you give up certain aspects of your life that you have before hung onto so tightly, you actually become more independent and feel a sense of freedom when you finally let go. After some resistance Chester did give in and very soon got to like the constant attention and care that he received from someone especially designated to assist him. He even became more inclined to make requests to a professional caregiver where before he might hesitate asking me to do something, thinking he would be bothering me "one more time." In the long run, Chester probably got more intense and constant attention from this hired person than I could have given him.

Next, I had to deal with my own reservations. I said that I didn't want a stranger living in my home and interfering with our family privacy. But when there was no alternative, I designated a certain area of our condominium to be considered all mine. I insisted on my little room to be "my little room," no matter how small it was. It was cute, little, and private. I used it for my bedroom, my office, for my respite. It was totally my space. It worked for me.

Lastly, I rebelled, saying that it was impossible to find someone to live-in and do all that was necessary. It certainly was impossible, as long as I didn't try. However, it was not unfeasible, and not even difficult once I made an effort. First I called the Senior Citizen Center in our area. They supplied us with a group of applicants who were quite adequate for the caregiving job. In time I also hired people through agencies that deal strictly in caregivers, and I used the local classified ads as well. After interviewing several people, we were fortunate to find several loving, caring, and capable people who lived with us from time to time. I checked references extensively, and I wasn't embarrassed to ask a lot of questions and screen the applicants thoroughly. This time, I was the boss.

Besides assisting my husband primarily, they helped me run our household and became welcome companions for us both. Most important of all, I felt confident that when I left my home, my husband was safely in good hands. The care that Chester received from our live-ins was often of a quality superior to the help that I was able to give him because they were skilled and trained in the caregiving field and most important of all, not emotionally entangled.

Once I resolved the problem of additional help in the house, I found that I actually had more time to get to know Chester's illness better. While allowing my help to move closer to the situation, it was then possible for me to stand back and become more objective. I was then able to make a genuine effort to learn more about the disease and study the problems at hand as well as situations that could be expected in the future. Somehow when I was right on top of it I was too emotional to see the issues clearly. But I found that understanding the illness itself, independent of the patient, was a crucial step in the caregiving process. It permitted me to anticipate certain parts of the illness with neither fear nor surprise, and more than anything it gave me the opportunity to plan for the future.

After seeing this situation through, I felt that I had taken important steps toward making decisions for carving out my own destiny. Not only did solving this huge problem aid me physically and emotionally, I also felt that I was able to pry open the gates of my prison. I was able to take back some of the control I thought had vanished, and suddenly this new freedom introduced an avalanche of additional solutions. A good portion of my life was now returned to me, and this time I could enjoy it.

In dealing with this massive challenge, I learned that even though I might lose control from time to time, as long as I stayed in there and had the fortitude to "just say no" to defeat, I found ways to live in the solutions of our problems.

My own health was the next important factor that I had to consider. I realized that I had a body that needed attention too, and it is not unusual for a caregiver also to suffer ill health along with the primary sick person. So I got a check-up by my own physician and made sure I was in top physical condition. Once my problems started turning into solutions, I wanted to be ready for the good times that I hoped would follow.

First of all, I took a good look at myself in a full length mirror. "No matter what, you've got to lose those fifteen extra pounds that you've been hanging onto," I shrieked at myself.

It was no secret that I had been eating constantly while watching TV, and more than anything else, I had overeaten from just plain loneliness. Nervousness and depression were not excuses anymore. No matter how hard I tried to make my heart happier through my tummy, somehow, the joy never reached my heart. It got stuck somewhere around my "middle," only increasing my depression. Strangely, when I was thin, I could handle my burdens easier. I used to joke that I wouldn't notice "if the house burnt down" if I were thin. Of course that wasn't true, but when I binged on food and added unnecessary sugar and carbohydrates to my digestive system, my metabolism was affected, which changed my state of mind and moods. More than ever, at that time I needed a healthy diet.

Instead of sitting down in front of the TV after dinner, I went for a two-mile walk in the early evening; and in the morning I got up a half-hour earlier and enjoyed the beginning of my day with a walk—summer, spring, or fall. I found it was a wonderful time to meditate, talk to myself, work out problems and solutions quietly, and have the fun of planning new goals. These were wonderful, private moments to think about the exciting things that I was not afraid to dream about anymore. Not only did I feel more like living, the exercise made me look like I wanted to live, and soon I even liked the way I was living. Taking care of the body is tremendously important as it also keeps one mentally fit, besides ensuring good health. As I built up the physical aspect of my exercise routine, whatever depression I had began to dissipate, and in addition, my cardiovascular health improved along with my total general health.

Continuing in my new regime, I found my way to adult classes in the local high school in my area. I entered a yoga and meditation class which greatly benefited my mental state. And before I knew it, I joined the aerobics group which worked on my mind and body too. Many classes sounded like fun. There was even a stress-relieving class. But by this time, I didn't need it. Hooray!

Needless to say, my pal in the full-length mirror encouraged a whole new look for me. I splurged on manicures, pedicures, facials, and of course professional hair styles. I found that the little tender loving care of my own physical self outside miraculously created the boost that I needed to help fix my insides.

As I put my free time to good use there was no doubt that I could feel and see the spirit of my world changing before my eyes. When I started taking care of myself, not only did I look and feel better, but I unknowingly transferred my focus from Chester and his illness to me and my own healthier life. I began at last to share the stage with my husband rather than helplessly sitting in the audience. As a result, I generally felt more deserving of a good life and automatically developed more self-worth along the way. I soon not only felt healthier, but in a short time, when I walked into a room, experienced a confidence which made me feel like I was somebody important. Although these solutions were only the beginning of the groundwork for my new life, they gave me the hope that I could someday become the woman of my own dreams.

# 8

## *Let's Face the Music and Dance*

### *Getting It All Together*

Once I began a new way of life, the music played more clearly in the background and I felt a lighter tempo guiding me to a new, healthier lifestyle. Life moved with a rhythmic flow when at last I reached out for additional assistance and incorporated various forms of help into my daily routine.

As my network of solutions expanded, I enjoyed the fun of bringing everything together. Positive elements were added to the circle of my support group, and I was greatly relieved to find that I didn't have to dance alone anymore. Though the pace was difficult at times, the new network of strength appeared as a ring of dancers holding my hands and bracing me as I whirled through the problems that confronted me.

A small group of loyal benefactors rallied around and consistently raised my spirits, providing the emotional stability that I so badly needed. I knew that I could go to these people with absolute trust, and that they would offer me unconditional love, strength, positive direction, and "strokes." Censoring every issue before I approached my confidants wasn't necessary, for they gave me the confidence to know that they were going to love me as much at the end of each conversation as at the beginning. I knew that I was in safe hands when, in spite of the fact that even though sometimes I recognized myself as repetitive, boring, and tedious, my friends were willing to listen because they understood my deep need to share my inner voice. When I could count on so little else in life to keep me going, I knew that my immediate support group had the resilience to combat my insecurities and would offer me the right answers when I could not even think for myself. Countless times my friends listened to me without having a silent alarm go off signaling a need for me to stop. They knew my life was on the line and they cared.

Ironically, I learned the lesson of patience from these dear ones. While paying close attention to me and my needs, unintentionally they taught me how to support and listen to someone else. They gave me instruction in the senses, teaching me to hear, see, and feel another person's pain from his outward cries of help, or perhaps merely from observing his silent agony. These were valuable lessons, and I am sure I could not have existed without their mindful and caring attention. Thus, as a result of my mentors' caregiving to me, I learned to be a more patient and untiring caregiver to my husband.

In addition to my own personal support group, nontheless, I found that I also needed a more structured support system of some kind, as well. I knew that it was unfair to burden my friends with questions they were not equipped nor qualified to answer. A productive working relationship within a formal group thus eventually became a valuable life-line in solving many problems.

Even though I knew this was an important element in my survival, for a long time I chose not to sit around a table and discuss my problems and listen to others with similar ones because of a bad incident that I had experienced. While at my lowest emotional ebb, just before the revelation at the crucial Christmas party in 1991, I innocently went to a support group to seek help and guidance, hoping to find ways to keep my own life intact. But the members seemed to dwell only on the source of their problems and not on trying to solve them. They appeared to be empty, lifeless, saddened by the hard blows that life had dealt them and embittered by the task laid upon them of healing everyone except themselves. The participants were angry that they hadn't allowed themselves choices and they were resentful that they had allowed the illness they were dealing with to trap two lives, one being their own. In addition to feeling torn down the middle and lacking completeness on either side, they felt only their own despair as the core of their lives.

My own dear friends had urged me to go to the support group and ask the fellow sufferers at the meeting how I could simply live my own life again and begin to enjoy some happiness for myself. My friends thought surely these folks with experience could help me. I did, too. With the best of intentions I got myself together and found my way to the meeting. In the most basic of terms, I asked the members of this group to tell me how they had managed to continue living their own lives while still caring for their spouses for so many years. I sat at the table the whole meeting, crying, feeling very much alone, and in the deepest emotional pain I had ever experienced. Finally when it was my turn to speak I begged the caregivers around the table to offer me some assistance, telling them that I felt as if I were dying a slow and tortuous death. I thought certainly they would have the answers since they had been through what I was then trying to endure.

"Please," I cried, "please tell me how to have a life. How can I save my own?" I took a breath, "My friends said you would know how I can get my life back," was all I could get out. I felt so weak, almost faint. I tried so hard to hold back my sobs.

The faces watching me looked lifeless, the eyes sad. Empty. The initial response was a sickening silence. After a lengthy pause which seemed to go on forever, one pathetic soul stared at me with amazement and answered softly, "We never had one."

I looked questioningly at all of them, not comprehending the answer, and innocently asked once more. "How can I begin to live my own life again and enjoy some happiness for myself?" I paused, as I was sure I had incorrectly heard their response. Then added, "You never had what?"

Once again the group leader repeated the answer that I did not understand the first time, and she said in the deadest voice I had ever heard, "We never had a life and neither will you!" Knives pierced my heart. I felt sick to my stomach. I ached with pain.

I pulled back, shocked. Somehow I knew there had to be an answer to this horrible problem. Though I wasn't sure at that point how to find it. I only knew that it had to exist. I understood as well as anyone how easy it would have been to give up and take the easier way out by running away from either the unknown or the ever-unfolding present. But I was absolutely certain that I could not run away from my troubles any longer. I'm not sure if my inner strength at that crucial moment came from the confidence in my experience of overcoming my previous problems in life, feeling the strength of my friends who were behind me, or if I just felt my own intense need for self-preservation.

What I did know was that I was sure I did not want to join that sad, demoralized group. Suddenly I felt that the table they were gathered around was the symbol of the separation between the happy life I hoped would exist "out there" for me and the hopeless group that I was watching.

At that very instant I knew that I could, and indeed would stand up to my own crises and fight through each terrible situation just as if I had Parkinson's disease myself. In that moment of clarity I realized that it was impossible for me to live the rest of my life looking as if my face was etched in stone and that my heart had been replaced by a machine. Even though I didn't know how it would come to pass, I knew then that I had to live my life differently from the rest of the people around that table. Most important of all was that I knew that I had to decide if I were to live, or to die. I made an instant, on-the-spot decision. To live. But I knew that I had to do it my way. At this crucial point I chose to move forward instead of retreating into a life of reclusive, deep loneliness.

My mind raced as I stood up and leaned on the table. I stared back at them. And though my heart felt frail and my knees felt like butter, I gathered all of my strength, and the next thing I knew, I bolted toward the door. Before I could think about what I had just heard from those very disheartened people, I turned to the ten sets of eyes silently awaiting my response. I sobbed words that rang in my ears for the rest of my caregiving life, "I want to live! I'll find my life! *My way!*"

I ran out and closed that door behind me forever.

I certainly did not forget the marriage vows that I made with Chester twenty-seven years earlier when I said, "for better or for worse," but I felt there had to be other alternatives to completely forgoing the rest of my life and watching the slow disintegration of both of our lives together. I had been through far too much in my life and had managed to emerge from each crisis finding a solution. I was still fairly young and healthy, and most important of all I knew that there were some tunes left for me that could take me to the dance floor. In any event, the experience with the saddened group made it even more clear that I did need help from a formally structured support group. It was essential however, that I find one that felt comfortable and right for me. I categorically did not want to feel more depressed at the end of a session than when it started. So after some deliberation and discussion with my friends, I decided to start a support group of my own with an upbeat rhythm, and it would be one that would only deal with exploring and sharing positive and productive means of coping with illness.

The group was to be called, "Living with Solutions."

Just the excitement of thinking I could start an upbeat group was an elevating experience and raised my spirits enormously. When I began having an interest in other caregivers welfare's, I immediately began to feel better myself. And as I started to become more involved with others in need, I coincidentally discovered there was a large roster of other genuinely productive support groups available as well. Once I began thinking along positive lines, new elements automatically came into my life and redirected my downward thoughts.

At this point, before I actually got "Living in Solutions" off the ground, I coincidentally was fortunate to find an already organized chapter of a wonderful organization which dealt with support in a positive manner. The Well Spouse Foundation came to my rescue when I was sure that I would have had to do it all by myself. This support group had a philosophy most akin to my own in that it emphasized the addition of quality to a problem-riddened life, and stressed dealing with answers to these problems; not endlessly ruminating about them. In addition to problem solving, the Well Spouse Foundation practiced learning how to play and have fun. The meetings at Well Spouse were focused on the caregiver and not on the person in their care. Though they were formally structured, each chapter was run by well spouses with no particular qualifications, and they were planned in an easy-to-follow format. However, qualified visitors spoke at meetings and offered valid suggestions for solving various legal and financial problems that arose. I felt a certain safety knowing that I was receiving appropriate advice from professionals with valuable experience. The speakers at the meetings were chosen with the idea of helping the caregiver and lifting their spirits while addressing numerous situations requiring professional answers.

Discussing problems is not always a solution to them, and sometimes the discussion of the very problems feeds the issue and fertilizes negative growth. Therefore, I had to discriminate carefully as to the benefit I received. I discovered there was a fine line dividing positive and negative thoughts. It was helpful to sit and discuss my problems for two hours, but I realized that I also listened to other people's problems for the same two hours. For me it was beneficial to listen to what I perceived as wise and successful solutions for the duration of the meeting, as is done in Well Spouse Foundation meetings, rather than focusing on the weightiness of every negative permutation of a "can you top this" situation in many support groups. I had to remind myself that support groups were supposed to be just what they were called. Their goals were to support one's morale and not lower it.

Well Spouse Foundation was so similar to my own idea for "Living in Solutions," and since they were already well established, I gladly let WSF guide me in my support group needs. However, I will always be thankful for the first thoughts of "Living in Solutions," for it gave me my first ray of hope and showed me that when you really try to help someone else, you indeed help yourself. And this all can be accomplished with an uplifted spirit.

Next, my personal support system was greatly enhanced by the good fortune of my finding a wise and understanding therapist. Alice guided me in making major decisions and dealing with problems as they came into being. She held my hand as I walked through many slippery paths and often was the one person in whom I placed total confidence. All in all, she helped me find a safer place over some very tough spots that I had to endure. I required a great deal of attention at the beginning of my new life, and I needed to know I could feel emotionally selfish and completely secure for at least one hour during the week. Alice explained to me that the feelings of isolation and loneliness that I felt were not unusual for a person in my position, and she encouraged me to find alternatives to my living pattern if I wanted to. Mainly I learned that there was neither a right nor wrong way for me to be happy, but only my way would work for me.

Suddenly my responsibilities seemed less like burdens and more like challenges to be met. I got to the point where I called myself a fireman, knowing that I could extinguish each problem that originated. I simply stopped falling apart and ceased feeling like I wanted to lock myself in a room and scream.

Though these therapy sessions were centered around my welfare, the results were not entirely self-serving. In fact, they turned out to be quite the contrary. As I began to feel my safety expand, the stronger I acted. Soon I began to feel happier and less worried. Before I knew it, I found myself more aware of other people's needs, and then, without question, more patient, able, and enthusiastic in taking care of Chester.

The evolution of my recovery in therapy took me up from deep depression to more level plateaus, and then a balanced emotional life. Therapy introduced me to the experience of quality times with Chester as they were happening. I learned to share the benefits of my therapy with him, and to enjoy many more of our days together. We experienced a loving sensitivity between us because of what I learned, and I became proud and happy to be by his side as I wheeled him in his wheelchair through the shopping mall or when we stopped for lunch in the bright sunshine along the busy boulevard. I was content with our moments together.

Another key element in my recovery to emotional security was that I developed a friendship with a trustworthy ladyfriend with whom I spoke freely, comfortably, and regularly. We built a continuous, solid rapport between us, so that whenever I had a major problem, it felt normal for me to call her. She basically knew what was going on in my life, therefore when something important came up or when I just needed a sounding board, she already had the fundamental details in place. The level of my problem was never the issue, but rather I was secure in knowing that I could discuss whatever was bothering me, even though it mightn't be of major critical proportions. It felt comfortable to approach Edythe for any issue, since I had established a pattern of daily contact. Discussing my problems with a friend with whom I was positive I could trust saved my life countless times. I was sure that Edythe really cared for my welfare and I always felt absolutely confident that she loved me unconditionally. This allowed me to speak openly and honestly on any subject and I always knew she was on my side no matter what we were discussing. Best of all, our relationship gave me the confidence to go out and increase my circle of friends with other women and to truly enjoy these new friendships.

Lucky for me, I fell into the arms of some very bright and caring women. They loved me gently and loved me tough, but they were always there when I needed them. I learned the importance of being thoroughly honest and realized that this was not the time to play games. There's no value in looking good on the outside and dying on the inside. My friends knew when I was hurting, and how good it felt when I became unburdened by shedding outward pretenses. I found joy in the gift of security that they brought me and wondered how I would have survived at all without them.

My support system stabilized, the energy flowed, and more solutions soon started to dance in my mind. Though it was hard to look beyond the sad affairs that stared at me daily and even think of having a good time, I felt the excitement of developing new interests for my own pleasure once the healthy juices began to stir. On the one hand, I was depressed and worried about the poor health of my loved one, and on the other, I could not restrain the desire to go out and live my life again. I reminded myself that I was dealing with long-term care, not the frame of reference required for brief, or even relatively short-term illnesses. The problems and the solutions are entirely different for catastrophic and terminal illnesses rather than for illness of a chronic nature. The doctor told me that Chester's illness would continue to progress and could go on for many years, perhaps indefinitely. My recovery all at once exploded, and I could not wait for an appropriate time to begin the continuance of my own life. There was no alternative left for me, but to live. My way!

The sad realities that had torn me apart for so long and had eaten at my insides until I could no longer bear the pain, made me realize that I had already earned this small break in my life. We had at last built up to the point where the recovery had to be for me. Not knowing how my life would change or how these changes would be manifested,

I unconsciously let go and it all seemed to happen. When I was brave enough to face up to the facts before me, my spirit found a new energy, and all at once my heart began to dance.

# 9

## Begin the Beguine

### Reentering Society

From the cradle was where I started to live my life. Like a baby, I crawled first, then walked and ran along my own path, until I finally began to dance. After I once accepted that it was okay to start, the choices were easy. The decision was all mine, and all I had to do was decide what made me happy, and do it. I merely had to think about my own interests and desires. It was almost as if someone had waved a magic wand over my head and said, "It's your turn now, get started and have some fun."

This was an assignment that I couldn't fail, because I was the only one who knew the right answers for my life and maybe for the first time in a long time I did what pleased me. The process of thinking in self-seeking terms took some getting used to, because up until then I had not answered my own needs, and as a result had not yet experienced how great it felt to have my own desires placed on top of the totem pole instead of near the bottom. Caregiving took on a new meaning in that I began with taking care of the caregiver—*me*.

Many exciting discoveries were made. I discovered that time was on my side. My future had been restored to me in the form of the present, without the normal limits of measured progress. I judged my advancement now by the happy days that I accumulated at the time, and not by dragging out the baggage or my old notions of the past. I was in no rush except to add pleasure to my life. The gift of time was handed to me and I attempted to put it to good use. I tried to choose wisely, but the important thing was, I chose.

Enjoyment really began when I actually crept into the world. Though I felt somewhat intimidated, I cautiously took my initial steps into a familiar environment where I thought I would feel more confident. As I had been an avid tennis player for many years I reentered the tennis realm, hiding behind the security blanket of this familiar sport. Though I wasn't a newcomer to a sporting interest, the difference now was in my attitude as I approached the court. I didn't care about the outcome of the game as much as the level of enjoyment I experienced while playing. I joined social tennis tournaments as a single looking for a partner where I could meet new people. This proved to be a great deal of fun. I met a lot of new people and started to concentrate on laughter and jokes on the court instead of only trying to win. I knew by taking this first step I was already one set ahead.

Even though I felt a confidence around the tennis court and enjoyed that part of my life very much, things really began to open up when I developed an interest in a new sport, golf. First of all, it was something completely different to me. Learning to hit the ball was a new venture that consumed me mentally and physically, and the learning process, though frustrating, left me feeling relaxed and satisfied. I found the details of the sport to be highly mental. While I was acquiring the skills to play golf, I found myself completely absorbed in each movement of the swing and the need for total concentration on what I was doing. Later, as I began to understand and feel somewhat adequate in playing the game, I became overwhelmingly caught up in the challenge. I found it is true that one can only do one thing at a time, and while I was concentrating on my checklist of instructions to hit the ball on the golf course, I somehow did not think about the slate of problems waiting for me at home.

I found myself magnetically drawn to this new focus and my mind was channeled toward something other than my problems. Furthermore, it introduced me to a whole fresh group of people who were soon to become my friends. Here is where I reached a new plateau. I became known, liked, and socially accepted for myself, and was no longer thought of primarily as someone's wife. I began thinking and feeling in a singular dimension, seeking companionship for myself with these new acquaintances. Bonds were automatically created with my new sport companions, and before I knew it I was on the way to building my own independence. Thus without being consciously aware of the dynamics of what was happening, I created a new enjoyment and purpose in my life.

This new condition of independence, however, also introduced me to a distinct set of problems with which I had to contend. I needed to draw boundaries in my life and move forward in a way that felt comfortable without neglecting any of my primary responsibilities to my husband.

Once that fact was secure in my mind, I realized that I was enjoying myself for the first time in many years. Indeed this pleasure produced an altered kind of excitement—a new kind of fun. Not obligatory fun. Instead, these were unique feelings never felt before. It was as though I needed to carefully tiptoe through the happy moments, afraid that if I acknowledged my own happiness too exuberantly it might go away.

"Can this be me? Are these feelings of fun normal? Do people really live like this, enjoying themselves? I mustn't say a word out loud or it will go away."

I was afraid that I might awaken and find it wasn't right for me to enjoy myself with these new and different, pleasant emotions. I had to have validation from someone. I questioned my girlfriend on the telephone that day.

"Debbie, wanna hear something crazy? I had some fun yesterday. Do you think it's okay?"

I heard her laugh on the other end of the phone, and she yelled back at me, "Of course it's okay for you to have fun," and then happily said, "Hooray!"

But I had to hear approval over and over again until I finally became accustomed on my own to expecting a good time. I learned that happiness is self-made and that the gratification of my life's blessings began with just an idea of pleasure.

Though it seemed less difficult to start off in the familiar territories of my sporting interests, I believe it was also easier for me to get out because I enjoyed the social background where sports were played. I was likewise less intimidated going by myself to a social function with a tennis racket in my hand or golf clubs on my arm, knowing everybody I would meet there was mainly interested in just having a good time. However, the important fact was that I forced myself to engage in social interaction with other people.

When I saw that these activities worked, I sat down with pen and paper and wrote down other possible interests where I might spend my time. As I began to investigate various forms of entertainment, I discovered that going to art galleries and looking at paintings and contemporary sculptures provided me enriching and relaxing moments. Upon leaving a gallery I realized that I had not worried the whole time I was viewing the works of art. That seemed like a miracle. I started to enjoy the study of art more and more, and after a time took part in a weekend art seminar excursion. I met fascinating and interesting people, and not only managed to enjoy myself, I also learned the finer points of a new kind of art and created one more valuable interest with which to engage. Most important of all, I discovered that I could stand on my own two feet in a completely fresh environment and felt comfortable doing so as I watched the birth of my new independence. This experience was heightened as I consciously found excitement in getting to know myself in a fresh context in a more mature phase of life.

The mental stimulation of a political group, various classes at the local high school and university in painting, sculpture, writing, computer, sewing, and business management were all on my list. Once I started thinking about it, I couldn't write fast enough. Even though I didn't do all the things I wrote down, each one was a mental diversion for the moment, and I knew the possibilities were available for me if I desired. And of course at the top of my list, were tap, ballroom, salsa, and Western dance classes. I found something especially relaxing in dance. The music nurtured my soul while the exercise healed my body, and the combination of the two seemed naturally to give a healthy release to my nervous system while offering great enjoyment. Since dancing is usually a pacesetter for a social mood it was a wonderful way to meet people as well. I found that people who like to dance are generally friendly and display a temperament that is not threatening. And best of all, I felt safe since dancers are mainly serious about the sport of dancing.

One day the travel section in the newspaper caught my eye. My mind immediately shifted to high gear when I realized I could use my Mileage Plus credit card for airline tickets. Hmmmmmmm!

I started charging everything that I bought on my Mileage Plus card. That included food, clothing, cleaning, gasoline—even visits to medical doctors and prescriptions. I couldn't believe that Chester's doctor bills helped send me to New York at Christmas time. What a wonderful way to go, and a perfect solution to my need for escape, fun and recreation. For me travel was a great diversion. It offered a change of environment, and it also extricated me from the weighty atmosphere that caregiving unfortunately brought into my life. At the same time, Chester was able to enjoy a diversion and spent time with someone else, too. These periods of respite were absolutely crucial as an antidote for the isolation that the illness produced for both of us. I am convinced that this kind of nourishment let me survive the whole length of the illness, and at the same time we watched the psychological environment in which we were living improve before our eyes.

There came a time when I had to be brave enough to re-evaluate various forms of the joint life style I had been used to sharing with Chester, which included traveling together. After I adjusted to living more on my own, I realized that the elimination of certain activities weren't deprivations at all, and the changes actually added quality to my life and to Chester's as well. Indeed it was sad that I no longer had my husband for my traveling companion, but I considered carefully that we were better off with me traveling solo. At its best, traveling can be difficult and stressful, and I had to judge the benefits for both of us. The most magnanimous and generous decision of all was to allow Chester to remain at home with the comforts of familiar surroundings, food, medical equipment, and his trusted routine. Instead of feeling guilty for taking a trip by myself, I realized that guilt was more justifiable if I encouraged him to go with me. Ultimately, it was a relief for him not to have to go. And once I got over the "shoulds" in this situation, I took the money I would have spent on his part of the trip and paid for some really good extra home health care for him. I did us both a favor by going alone.

The momentum built up and my shopping list for a happier life grew with my new excitement for living. Many wonderful things to do appeared when my attitude changed, and I became willing to take some risks to reach my goals. I joined a chapter of the Sierra Club and on beautiful days hiked in the mountains above our ravishing desert and got in touch with nature's wonderment. Nothing was as peaceful as watching the gentle radiance of the golden hew of the sun setting behind the purple mountains in the vista. The warmth of the pastoral environment was a treasured gift that never would have been mine to enjoy had I not ventured out of my emotional cocoon. A morning watching the breaking of dawn or an evening at sunset were far more satisfying than spending the money on trips to the psychiatrist's office.

I became an active member of the local museum and the philharmonic group at our music center; and I even had some fun in an amateur drama production. The main idea was focusing on another endeavor instead of my woes. Believe it or not, when I concentrated on memorizing lines for a play or simply relaxed and listened to every chord in a Chopin piano concerto it wasn't possible for my thoughts to travel back home.

And the lineup continued. Guitar and piano lessons soon moved toward the top of my list, along with history and psychology classes at the local college. Once I captured the essence of my program, I had the courage to learn to do just about anything I wanted. How much simpler it was when I turned away from the goal of perfection. The object of these exercises was not just to fill time—instead they helped me start to live my life with gratification and fulfillment. Since I wasn't trying to win any prizes I didn't have to be an expert at whatever I did. Engaging with the outside world and having fun were my final rewards. And there were many.

At about this time I thought that a part-time job might be enjoyable. While helping to staunch the financial drain, it also moved to rebuild my self-worth. But I had to make sure not to forget that my main objective was my pleasure, and the monetary gain, though helpful, was secondary. The goal was not to build a financial empire for my future, but to brighten the spirit of my heart in the present. Long-term goals were only important if they also offered immediate psychological rewards. Whatever job I thought about, I made sure it included a forum for meeting and talking to people. It was fun to help out temporarily in the golf and tennis pro shop; my dentist always needed an extra hand; and the book store in the mall was an excellent place to work, as it was always filled with interesting people.

At this point I feel I must address the "M" word, as undoubtedly, money and one's financial position is a serious issue in any caregiver's life. Though a major part of my success seems to have been helped by my lack of extreme financial problems, the truth of the matter is that I had been victorious over the obstacles that I had to transcend only because I practiced what I described here. We did not have unlimited funds to be used foolishly, and actually, the victories were not contingent on money in any way. In fact, before I reached a happier emotional state, I spent many depressed, sad times while garnering lucrative financial gains. Money and financial position never realistically were a common denominator of my moods, mobility and state of mind. The fact is I am in close contact with unhappy rich people with emotionally poor attitudes, and financially poor people with rich and happy states of minds. It is not uncommon to be rich in material wealth and have a bankrupt soul. I readily admit that it was easier to play all of the above games being financially sound, but with the high costs of nurses, doctors, hospitals, and general medical treatment, I honestly did not know what our financial situation would be down the line, and that was always a condition that provoked worry for me. However, my state of mind improved only because I was willing to take some chances regardless of money. More important is the fact that this learning experience gave me the chance to fill up my emotional bank for my psychological security. Money did not buy me inner peace or the smile in my heart that I needed to carry on my life in a happy manner. When funds were limited, I needed to be more creative. But I found that it could be done.

There came a time when I simply refused to sit around any longer feeling unhappy and sorry for myself. The familiar lump in my throat was intolerable and I just couldn't wait quietly by the side while I watched the rest of the world enjoy life. I knew that it was time for me to take charge of what life was available to me and to participate in the decisions of my destiny. I took the advice of my trusted friends and chose to "lighten up." And as I took heed of their suggestions, I saw that the only person who ever stood in the way of my enjoyment of life was me. Instead of giving in to a hopeless depression, I found that I had been on the brink of catching a rainbow of hope and that a new and most exciting part of my life was right there waiting for me. So once I put my fears aside, I began to begin the satisfying rhythm of living.

# 10

## Now We're Starting to Swing

### The World Hears our Needs

When I stepped outside the shadow of the illness, I developed the strong desire to discover more about the entire scope of the hideous malady that afflicted us. Once I began to read and hear from the news media reports that the world was developing a new interest in the physically challenged and their special needs, in my mind I drifted to the other side of the dance floor where the music began to swing. New hope that I was not alone in my dilemma gave me the encouragement to further investigate our problems and support the improvements for the betterment of the disabled, and now also the caregiver.

The pace of change was often uneven and sometimes wearisome and painfully frustrating, but as in the learning of most new routines, ideas are transformed from abstract images into concrete realities in slow increments. The requests for aid on the part of the physically challenged had to be broken down into small, measured solicitations, so that society would accept the learning process and help realize our goals, rather than run from us in fear. We could not rush the tempo of the changes that we desired, and more often than not, our efforts had to be expended over and over again until at last we succeeded.

Trudging along through the years, we were fortunate to watch the progression of the unpopularity of discrimination and the disintegration of its malignant characteristics. The struggle for equal rights over various health categories, that had been a part of our lives for so long, finally prevailed. People in wheelchairs banded together with the mighty force of Samson, and with one strong unified voice called for help, support, and justice. The physically challenged spoke out fearlessly as a unit, with pride, until they could finally hear their own words echoing back down the halls, "Give us the dignity we deserve, the help that we are entitled to, and we will be a promising force in our communities." The world was shown what the term "courage" really meant when the disabled lined up in their wheelchairs in official buildings, and entered in political forums. They were more aware of the urgent need to cause change than they were of their own inabilities, and they sat and waited until they were heard.

Lawmakers in Washington, D.C. finally listened to their message as the many wheelchairs filled the hallways of buildings where crucial decisions are made. After many painful and difficult lessons, society finally began to listen, respond, and eventually to awaken to our needs.

The unity of the physically challenged and their peaceful demonstrations resulted in an examination of the disabled's cause by decision makers and was also a catalyst for change in public opinion. As wheelchairs continued to roll along to higher places, the combined voice of the disabled became more audible and the momentum increased. Soon the isolated feelings that illness produces were replaced by a common cause. The unfounded notion that a handicapped person is different was dissipated by knowledge of vast numbers of handicapped that surveys ultimately uncovered. Experts estimate that there are millions of people in the U.S. suffering from various forms of debilitating and chronic illnesses—Parkinson's and Alzheimer's disease, cardiovascular disease, diabetes, multiple sclerosis, arthritis, and stroke, to name only a few.

No longer are the physically challenged and disabled looked upon in our communities as different or threatening to others' welfare. Society has learned well the lesson that people who are distinct are neither better nor worse than another, but are entitled to equality in all areas of their lives.

The striking phenomenon in recognizing the immense numbers of suffering people in our midst is the realization that two people are involved in a single illness, a patient and a caregiver. Thus, came recognition of the part we caregivers play in the illness. However, when we look back to the evolution of our crusade for equality, we had to be painfully honest in our thoughts and actions. How could we expect society to treat our disabled equitably with the rest of the physically healthy among us when even we, who loved our dear ones deeply, still treated our care person a shade differently from the rest of the world? Somehow we had to examine our own deeds and notice the messages we were sending out. We had to understand that men and women need to be treated with the respect of adults, and that children have to be handled with the extra care that they require. But in every case, the caregiver must build a storehouse of patience in order to offer the care person the dignity he needs in order to weather the illness. Of course, this is easier to say, than to do.

As in most significant gains, painful lessons preceded notable improvements. The stronger and healthier began to comprehend more about the needs of the needy, and those who were blessed with strength and power reached out a hand to the less fortunate. We caregivers who were fighting for our own lives were at the same time educated in finding ways to make our lives a little more tolerable. Slowly we became adept in grabbing whatever lifeline was sent our way. And as time went on, we felt increasingly confident to demand more and more of the goodness and welfare that our society could provide in assisting the disabled, which they rightly deserved. Although it seemed slow and a long time in coming, great strides were made on behalf of the disabled, and most importantly, the groundwork was laid for even greater advancement for the disabled cause.

The Disabled Persons Act of 1990 was the culmination of many years work done by our mentors. Though it was only the beginning of concrete measures written for the welfare of the disabled person, it was also a strong eye-opener to the general public, to become willing to look upon the disabled as equal contributors to our society. It opened up many opportunities for expansion of our lives by insuring physical mobility and safety in the public sector as well as offering regulations and standards for opportunity in the workplace. Most public buildings and schools are now equipped with handicap facilities, as are offices, stores, restaurants, malls, hotels, public transportation, and sidewalks. The physically disabled person can most often be assured that when they leave the curb, more than likely they will now reach the other side of the street safely, and when entering a building, they will not be given an impossible course of physical obstacles to overcome.

The Act for Disabled Americans stressed guidelines for leading the way to equality in jobs, and specifically fought discrimination in the hiring process. The physically challenged person's work is measured and judged now by how well the work is done, and not by who is doing it. However valuable the deeply appreciated benefits the program introduced, the significance of the educational tone that it established in the minds of the general public must not be overlooked. As with any new advance, the changes began with thought and courage. Only then was progress possible. We celebrate now the strides made, knowing that the seeds for an easier future were planted.

During my own experience as a caregiver, I devised shortcuts from lessons I learned that aided me in the very difficult and seemingly impossible tasks with which I was faced. Many of these points are directly the result of the country's response to our outcries and, put to practical use, they have become solutions for everyday problems. I call these ideas "Handicapped Ease," as they made my life a little easier.

One of the first things I did was I obtained a "handicapped person" placard which I placed on the dashboard of my car. It signals that the car is operated by or for a handicapped person and allows special privileges in the laws for parking and otherwise. This little sign is ordered by the doctor and provided by the Department of Motor Vehicles. It indicates a handicapped driver or passenger in the car, and permits parking in designated handicapped-only spots, allows them to ignore certain time restrictions on parking zones, and makes it unnecessary to feed the parking meters. This specifically grants the right to take extra time on parking spaces on public streets and enables one to park a car closer to entrances, exits of malls and shopping centers, and elevators. You can drive up to self-serve pumps in service stations and the management will put gas in your car and give full service if desired. This may seem like a small thing, but more than once I didn't want to leave Chester in the car alone and the only service stations available in the area were self service. I simply honked my horn, showed my placard, and let the service attendants know that I needed assistance. We received only pleasant responses. In all, the placard's functions simplified our mobility.

When we went to a restaurant, I called ahead and mentioned that a member of our party was disabled and that we wanted a suitable table for a wheelchair, up front if possible, so we wouldn't have to walk through the entire restaurant. People in general are extremely kind today to handicapped people, and it seems as if everybody wants to be the one asked to help. As a result, we received a warm reception at the restaurant door as they awaited our arrival, and in cases like these, I liked being different. For many years Chester's chair had to be pushed in and pulled out from the table since he was no longer able to negotiate this task. I struggled to do this job though it was very difficult, and onlookers' stares made me feel embarrassed as well. I felt that everyone was noticing my strained activity, as it was simply too difficult for me to pull that kind of weight gracefully.

Finally, after too many stares in restaurants, I realized how to overcome this problem. Again, a simple problem was solved by a simple solution. When seated in a restaurant, I quietly asked the maitre d' or waiter to assist my husband. And from then on, we were pampered, all our needs graciously met, and the service we received was always better than normal. When we were ready to leave the restaurant, I asked again for the same assistance. Not only did I feel like a lady, I also went home without a pulled back and minus a little extra stress that I carried around for too long.

Heaven knows we have to carry some of the weight and baggage of the illness, but I got rid of what I didn't need. Also, I learned that if I ever needed help, I simply asked for the manager and always got a friendly and helpful response. In the event that Chester needed to be assisted in the restroom, I asked the manager of the restaurant if he would kindly provide a busboy or someone to accompany Chester, or if Chester's nurse was with us, then I asked for permission for her to enter the men's restroom with him. It is a lot less uncomfortable or embarrassing to ask, rather than to try to either wait or manage alone with difficulty.

When we went to a public place with a parking attendant, I quietly asked the valet if he would assist me with the wheelchair. I learned over and over again that if I asked, I received help and assistance. Never was I turned down. More often than not, the valet took the wheelchair out of my car, helped place Chester in the chair and wheeled him inside the building for me. Now, that's service. I found that the magic word here was "*ask*." If an employee wasn't available, I asked a stranger to assist me. The response was always congenial, and the person I asked acted as if I had done him an honor to have been chosen to help. I learned to "ASK, ASK, ASK."

The same help is available at doctors' offices, parking lots, public buildings and stores. And at movies, we went directly to the front of the line. No one ever refused our genuine and sincere request: a simple, "Will you please give us some assistance?" At a theater or movie, simply, "May we please go right in?" Then, magic! In we went. The same is true for sporting events, or actually anything that produces a line or a crowd. As long as we're so popular and sought after today, then by all means, go for it. We deserve our share. I feel that for every request voiced by me, another handicapped person may be assisted by the public's new awareness of our needs.

When we traveled by airline, I requested a wheelchair ahead of time. I asked either my travel agent or our airline ticket consultant for this service, and there was a wheelchair and an attendant to push it waiting for us at the curbside when we arrived at the airport. I requested handicap service throughout our entire itinerary, and the help always added energy for both me and Chester. Internationally, we were whisked through identification and custom checks to the front of the lines. This kind of service extended our traveling life span a great deal. It certainly helped us when we could travel, and I look back with gratitude for these special services.

It was interesting and fun to investigate specialty boutiques and shops that are stocked with items specifically for the handicapped. There are stores that have objects designed especially to help one better cope with the limitations in the physically challenged person's life. They have unique suggestions for safer and easier methods for dining, sleeping, bathing, and entertainment. Items are available to assist one in every phase of daily living from getting out of bed, to getting dressed, walking, sitting, or breathing. Speaking clocks, and watches that have dials large enough to read can be purchased, along with kitchen facilities and eating utensils that are designed for easier usage by the disabled. There are beds and chairs that transport one's body in and out, making life a little easier, and a variety of clothing is available that makes getting dressed less cumbersome and difficult. The products we selected added practicality to our lifestyle and helped make a more comfortable and carefree existence.

Many of the items, though designed particularly for the handicapped, are extremely functional and helpful for anybody. Quite often when I chose an item to accommodate Chester's disability, I also enjoyed the benefits first-hand. These specialty stores are laid out in comfortable and realistic settings modeled after actual rooms. This offers the advantage of being able to try out an item in a real life setting.

Another important aid in our lives was the discovery of a day-care center for the chronically ill. One in our area is associated with the local hospital, and it enables the caregiver to leave the care person there for up to an entire day. The center gives the person lunch and provides him with entertainment and healthful facilities for a nominal charge. They are run by skilled and professionally trained people. This measure added a welcome diversion to Chester's routine and certainly enhanced my own.

At one point I was pleasantly surprised to find out that we were entitled to various forms of limited home nursing care by practical or registered nurses sent and paid for by Medicare. This service permitted a regular check on Chester's general condition. In addition, a physical and occupational therapist was also sent to our home for regular visits.

I found out the hard way how important it was to have complete knowledge of health insurance policy benefits, as some of the terms on our policy were vague and appeared misleading. When Chester was in a nursing care facility after his stroke, I was told that his supplemental policy to Medicare insurance would pay 80% of private duty nurses for him. However, the insurance company did not make it clear that I had to hire only registered or licensed practical nurses. Being unfamiliar with nursing care at the time and in an emotional and worried state, I was happy to have whomever the nursing registry sent out. Unfortunately, they sent us almost all certified nurse's aides rather than the appropriate nurses that would have activated my husband's insurance benefits. Needless to say, an unnecessary financial disaster occurred, and we were left with the unpleasant burden of paying 100% of twentyfour-hour-a-day private nurses for one month. If I had only asked…

Though it was painful to think about, I had to look at the future. Preparing for the weeks, months, or years ahead not only concerned Chester's future, but the effects of his illness and disabilities concerned my life as well. I looked into the availability of skilled nursing homes and facilities in my area before there was a crisis. While I had the time and was not emotionally pressured, I visited nursing homes that were likely candidates for Chester's future living. I familiarized myself with the available facilities, met the staff involved, had a meal in the dining room, and visited with the other patients in the public recreation rooms. I considered the ratio of helpers to patients and noticed the attitude toward the patients. In addition, I paid close attention to the location of the facility in regard to the proximity of my own home. I had to be aware of the convenience of others who would be potential visitors. Therefore, I chose one conveniently placed, considering potential visitors' travel time. This was not for the purpose of making the guest's life easier, but rather that the facility should be convenient enough so that Chester would indeed have visitors and company that he needed. It was much easier to look at situations such as these while I was not under extensive stress and pressures, and it made for better decisions as a consequence.

Finally when Chester's illness progressed to a critical stage, we received relief from a wonderfully helpful organization called "Community Hospice Care." At first I shuddered when I even thought of what the name implied. But when I was introduced to the lovely and qualified Hospice staff, I realized that once more the world had awakened to our needs. The program is designed to provide support for terminally ill patients and their families in the last six months of life, including special nurses and social workers sent out for one's personal assistance. The experience was a positive, beautiful, and helpful one, and I might add, it was entirely paid for by Medicare.

I had much to learn regarding the legal aspects of chronic illness entitled Elder Law, which deals with the handling and care of problems of the elderly. Although we were not eligible for financial assistance in nursing homes, I was advised on the possibilities of how best to place a person in a nursing home and still leave one's estate intact. And of course I found it generally efficient to research the various aspects of our wills and trusts. In these days of complicated legal standards, one can hardly do without effective legal counsel regarding such important issues. Once again, it was better to address these issues with a quiet and less troubled mind, before the crisis actually occurred.

Although my job as a caregiver was a difficult one, it was made easier by the use of the guidelines that I followed. Naturally, they did not smooth out the really tough road that I had to travel, but the way through it was simply made a little easier. As Chester's illness progressed and he became more incapacitated, there were times when I felt that I could not take the next step, though I knew as his caregiver I must continue, and I did.

Society's recognition of the caregiver and the disabled person opened up new, viable solutions and made some of our hopes come alive. But I believe that the most important stride taken was that the world has come to accept the physically challenged and their caregivers in daily life as just ordinary human beings like everyone else.

# 11

## May I Have This Dance

### Conquering Loneliness

After years of trying to cope with life's difficult tests, I was able at last to unite body and spirit and once more celebrate a new beginning. Even though my reconditioned physical self was ready to play its role in my new-found life long before it actually was called to task, I had to wait for just the right moment and the appropriate cue from its counterpart— my mind. Then, when both body and mind finally joined together in a healthy fashion, I began to feel the revival of fantasies blended with physical stirrings that I thought had been lost forever.

Repressed yearnings once more bubbled to the surface of my consciousness. Suddenly everything felt better. My limbs moved gracefully with lithe and limber gestures. Movements no longer were confined as I swerved and swayed to the imagined sounds of life's flowing music. Just as the unyielding emotional pain had been dominant for so long, constricting every natural inclination throughout the past decade, at this time a feeling of wholeness let me experience a new physical freedom enhanced by long forgotten instincts. Innocently, I watched the rebirth of the unification of my body, mind, and soul.

As before, my choices were limited. But this time I was aware of the irrepressible healthy gifts that were guiding me beyond my apparent limitations. I saw myself as a person with self-worth strengthened by the tough lessons I had learned. A completely different woman looked back at me in my mirror. I looked different because I was different. I rediscovered my very own existence. Not only did I feel it on the inside, I saw it beyond the surface as I peered into my now twinkling eyes before me. My skin had a new radiance and color and I felt an inner sparkle. It had been a long time since I had felt so alive.

When I moved I felt my body's youthful stride, and for the first time in years I was conscious of my femininity. I spun around and laughed with delight as I looked at my newly polished, bright red finger and toenails. Listening to the gurgling sounds in my belly, I felt a new bubble in my throat which told me my glands had stirred again. At the same time, I felt the flex of muscles that I thought had atrophied years before.

I looked in the mirror again and smiled, giving myself a knowing glance. I winked and told myself, "You made it, girl." I knew I had survived the greatest challenge of all—I had found myself once more. Besides, I knew that I had done so with pride and a restored hope for my future. The entry into this new phase of my life awakened feelings of strength and joy for which I had been waiting. The excitement for thoughts of living was overwhelming and I knew that the next time I heard the music playing I, too, would be dancing.

While contemplating my new philosophies, I had to decide between what felt right for me and what I thought looked right for the rest of the world. I could almost feel the sharp edge of a knife cutting away the shallow effects of my being, leaving only the most valuable qualities to enhance my new adventures. Quality was the single most important factor to play a role in this new part of my life.

Frequently we need to know that a flower has bloomed in someone else's garden before we can plant our own seeds. Not having had anyone else's experiences to draw upon, I had to make these difficult life decisions entirely on my own. I was not content with perhaps just stealing a little happiness. At this time, and being a dignified and respectable woman in my mid-fifties, I refused to sneak behind doorways to enjoy the life I felt I deserved. I wanted to live my life with a sense of pride, celebrating the new-found self-esteem that took so long for me to rebuild. Neither shame nor honors were in mind for living my own life; nor did I want to flaunt unorthodox behavior to attract unnecessary attention. I simply desired to grab the opportunity that awaited me.

I sought answers in every part of my brain, but the truth came to me in an instant when my psychologist, Alice, spoke to me in her office. I came to her confused, not knowing what to do. I asked for a response to my dilemma. I needed help dealing with the guilt I was feeling.

"It's okay to live your life your way. There's nothing wrong with it. Give it a chance, if you want it," she said.

Those were mighty words and proved to be the foundation for the meaningful existence that I began to live. Fully aware that one cannot "unring" the bell once it has sounded, I proceeded cautiously. Then, as I began to wend my way to a higher emotional plateau I found that the way up and out of a world marked by worthlessness became immensely exciting. Feeling this new healthy surge of life, I knew if I hung on to my fantasies they surely might come true.

The next stage of my life happened automatically as I became more relaxed psychologically and happier with the physical changes that I felt. At times it seemed almost as if my entire being had been transplanted into another body, and I began to feel a new strength and confidence I had not known before. It was hard for me to believe that I was the same person who left the room of the unhappy support group the preceding year.

But paradoxically, the more I accepted and became familiar with the positive transformation in myself, the more I became aware of a deep, enormous loneliness. The void was so strong that at times I could hardly deal with the pain that it produced. Even though the metamorphosis introduced great improvements in my life, it also opened up new, sensitive feelings that I had to learn to handle.

I spoke to myself almost in a dreamlike state. I talked to myself a lot in the past several years since oftentimes I was the only one there to listen. "I'm so lonely," I cried. "I'm lonely for the whole person inside of my brain. Where is the woman that I know can love with a heart filled with passion? Shhhh," I said, as if somebody could hear me. I kept quiet. I felt a stirring. I listened for a reply. There was only silence.

Before returning to reality I had a revelation that was very clear. Though I previously thought my loneliness could only be cured by another person, the uncontrollable desire to once more love myself became the strongest urge of all and the key to unlocking my solitude.

When I was deeply entrenched in my problems, many days were wasted harboring sorrow. Then, as time went on, my life became organized and happy, and my days were not devoted exclusively to depression and the related problems it caused. However, instead of feeling a new inner peace as my self-worth grew, the wellness simply charged my nerve endings and made me more acutely aware of the awful silence with which I had been forced to live.

Eventually, I started operating with a healthy mind and refused to accept that I had been placed on this earth merely to be an onlooker, without actively participating in life, when I had once felt so vital and important. It became intolerable to continue my life feeling like a voyeur. Watching. As my disturbances were resolved, awareness of a bare and naked reality arose from the depths to my conscious mind.

"I'm not sick anymore," once more I spoke out. "I'm ready to get up and go into the world and live again. Me too! Where's mine?" I insisted.

When the shade started to lift on life around me, I was too imbued with energy to stand by and just wait for my life to begin. I was eager for life's adventures. At the same time I was conscious of the pain of my own healing as I saw the contrast between the bright colors of a fully lived life and my own gray existence. Then, as the healing process took place I endured the scar formation that the wounds of loneliness caused.

When one is depressed and self-involved, it is normal to withdraw, but as one recovers from any illness it is natural to want to get up and re-enter the world. My own recovery felt like an actual physical incision that my body was trying to repair. I became healthier, and the desperate feelings attached to my previous isolation felt awkward because there was no longer need for me to withdraw. These feelings of habitual desperation thus ultimately developed into conflict with my healed emotions and healthier being, and caused my psyche to crave a more positive plane of existence.

I could almost visualize the various parts of my mind and body as they recuperated one by one. For so long I thought that I must tolerate everything. However, I began to live a richer life when I developed more courage to take the risks that were necessary for my life's changes. A very fine line divides the acceptance of what can and cannot be changed— having the actual courage to make changes in one's life where and when possible, and most importantly, having the wisdom to know the difference. I prayed for the serenity to adhere to the lesson in this beloved and well-known prayer from which the message was taken.

For a long time I had found it easier to take the less demanding route by blaming my loneliness on what I believed to be my destiny. I thought I could not change my world at all—I felt totally helpless. Eventually, I discovered it was possible to have a definite love and devotion to my husband, realize full acceptance of the responsibilities to him, and at the same time have the courage to change my life, while gathering a harmonious blend of life's gifts so that I was not lonely anymore.

It was true that I had added a fresh, colorful aura to my life by broadening my horizons and venturing out into the world. But it was not enough. I was still lonely, and apparently needed something more. In the past, business projects solved my boredom—however, at this time, I was not feeling the desire to regain my identity by reestablishing myself in the career world. I had stopped working to take care of Chester when his illness progressed, and I certainly didn't feel the need to prove myself any longer by professional pursuits. Many times in years gone by I had hidden behind a briefcase or title on a door to satisfy my ego. Part of my feeling useless later stemmed from the fact that I did remember what self-worth and recognition felt like so long ago.

At one time I had been totally obsessed with becoming independent. When I awoke in the morning, I tried to figure out how I could further my life without needing anybody at all. As a result of these frantic and unrelenting desires I did become successful in business, and outside approval finally ceased to be important to me as I rose to a station that allowed me to feel free and capable of making my own decisions.

Most of all, this successful lifestyle made me feel comfortable alone without needing anyone at all. I didn't require validation from the rest of the world to make me feel good, as I felt keenly satisfied with my accomplishments and independence. In fact, I did not need anyone for company socially as my business associates, in their own way, fulfilled my social needs. Of course, all the while, I always had my husband in the background of my life for support of any kind.

But this new gnawing at my sensitivities was distinct. At this time when I so badly wanted to share what I had emotionally with someone, no one was there. It was strange that when I achieved a comfortable stability with healthy ideals and values, I was alone. Because of Chester's illness, he had long ceased to be an emotionally giving companion and partner in our relationship. After fighting the symptoms of Parkinson's disease for twelve years or so, the evidence was overwhelming that he was losing the battle. It was clear that dementia had prevailed as hallucinations of imagined companions became his fanciful reality. Daily conversations with his unreal pals were all important to him and conclusive. He spoke to them as if they were actually in the room with him, and he perceived them to be his friends. He believed it all to be true. Finally, there was no longer a place in his life for me. His last defenses against the mental part of the illness were lost.

The medication for the illness, though it allowed Chester to have some temporary physical relief, oftentimes would exacerbate his frightening dementia. Neither result was tolerable. The choice was not an easy one. To medicate and to hope for a limited physical freedom but then having to hallucinate and live in this unreal world; or without medication to stiffen up and become rigid and immobile and hope to capture a minimal amount of coherent time. These were his only alternatives.

Even though at times he was lucid, he simply did not have the energy, after dealing with Parkinson's disease for so many years, to respond as a normal person. His primary function was simply to survive and be cared for. And I watched sadly, waiting for my own evil destiny to unfold. Thus I fell into deep depressions and the most intense feeling that I became aware of was "loneliness." I felt the longing for a nurturing of my heart and soul, and at the same time had come to the realization that I had denied some of my most basic needs.

I firmly believe that we attract what we want in life and unconsciously send out messages for the answers that we seek. Perhaps I wasn't really aware of the requests I projected, but I knew that I felt desolate and badly wanted a companion. I desperately wanted to have a pal with whom to laugh, talk, and share special moments. I wanted the common quality of a mate that most couples take for granted, as I had for so many years. I wanted a buddy to share my joy when I was happy or to hold my hand when I was sad. I wanted someone to finish my sentence when I couldn't think of the right word, one who just valued my thoughts. I wanted to think that I made a difference to one particular person in the world for the ideas I had to offer and to know for sure that I had a friend on my side against the world if I was mistreated. Sometimes I just needed to hear another voice of a friend.

I wanted to know that another's heart beat with mine when we listened to the gentle sounds of piano keys creating unforgettable melodies and we saw in each other's eyes tears of joy that the music evoked. I wanted a person to care if I was sick, and who wanted to see me healthy for my own benefit as well as his. I wanted an intimate relationship with a confidant knowing we would make up if we had an argument, and who also felt for me if I was hurt. I wanted a companion to join me in the beautiful outdoors, and hold my hand as we sat on a bench along the beach watching the sandpipers scamper on the water's edge.

I wanted a shoulder to lean my head on in a movie, and then to giggle with him later while we shared a pizza. I wanted a man to notice me when I got dressed up, and say, "You're gorgeous tonight, baby. You'll be the prettiest one there."

I wanted to say good night after the late news broadcast, and good morning when I smelled the aroma of hot coffee brewing. And most of all, when I heard the first bars of the music playing, I wanted to know that I would hear someone say, "Come on honey, let's dance."

Even though it seems I may have had more options than the average caregiver who provides approximately 93 hours of informal care per week to her impaired relative and is herself struggling to stay alive, these options did not become viable for me until I was entirely ready to go on to the next step. Being almost a generation younger than my husband (I was only 41 years old when Chester's illness was diagnosed), it made his deficiencies easier to accept as my own youthful physical condition helped me to cope. But ironically, because of my realative youth, I still had so many welled-up dreams and desires within me. So at the very same time this very positive factor became a negative, because I thought

I would have had the major part of my life ahead of me, for my own. And I did not.

The next phase then came easily, since at last I understood the deafening silence that filled my past. I had many years to justify my conclusion that the situation as it stood was no longer tolerable. I knew that I wasn't ever going to leave, walk away from, or avoid the responsibilities I had to my husband; nor was I going to disobey the moral part of the marriage contract to honor one another. I also recognized that I was on the verge of finding a way to move on with my own life.

I had consistently treated Chester with the highest esteem and respect, and I took pride in caring for him and his illness with dignity. In fact, I always was conscious of building his morale whether we were in public or the privacy of our own home, and I was extremely careful not to let anybody tamper with his emotional well-being. In essence, I exerted every effort to make him feel as comfortable as possible without exaggerating his difficulties, either to him or to the outside world. I loved him deeply and had the greatest concern for his welfare; and first and foremost, I saw to it that he always had the very best care possible. Yet while being fully conscious of all of this, I somehow managed to slip into a twilight zone, opening up cautiously and slowly to the outside world.

Ever so softly I heard the music being played off in the distance. Unsure of what lay ahead of me, I knew that my life was in the process of being reshaped. Though it was apparent that I was dealing with changes of my own, I didn't quite know how I would manage to cross the bridge to the other side of these transformations.

For a long time I needed validation from my personal support group. I called on friends and family to help me over the hurdle of feeling that I might be doing the wrong thing if I openly started to enjoy life and forget my sorrows. I had to have emotional assistance from people I could trust. I needed to feel their encouragement for me to go out, feel safe, and be happy. I began to listen when they spoke directly to me, and with the utmost sincerity yet so simply, I heard them say, "It's your turn now."

In fact, not only were my friends and family supportive of my newfound joys and experiences, Chester's family was the most supportive of all. His children were generous and reassuring in the encouragement they offered. It didn't matter whether or not that family vote of confidence stemmed from the fact that they knew I was doing an excellent job in the tough task of caring for their father, and that I needed to have some fulfillment in life if I were to be able to continue, or if they simply did not want the job of primary caregiver to be passed on to them. Whatever the reason, they gave me the support I needed and positively validated my feelings in a way necessary for me to live. This is not to say that I would have altered my course had they not agreed with my way of thinking, because at that point it would have been impossible for me to return to my previous unhappy existence. However, I felt a special peace of mind knowing that the people dearest to Chester were also dear to me.

So, armed with this great emotional support, I entered the doors of the future that I felt had been closed to me in the past. I suddenly felt as if I had been gifted with a part of life that I thought I never would experience. Continuing forward, I walked on with grace, dignity, and pride—without any preconceived motives, goals, or objectives. While I was still capable of having dreams fulfilled, I put one foot in front of the other and acted out my own hopes of capturing moments of happiness. At the same time I never dismissed the needs and desires of Chester.

In the beginning, balancing our schedules was difficult as I thought I needed to be in two different places at the same time. However, the more I practiced living my own life, the better I became at juggling my schedule and soon realized that I was actually spending more quality time with Chester than I had before. I planned my time with him when he was awake and lucid, and I left him when he was asleep or incapacitated by his illness. As a result, I felt refreshed and revitalized by the quality of fulfillment added to my life that I received away, and I was a happier care person to Chester when I returned.

The difficulty was that our schedules were not always perfectly synchronized. The care of a chronically ill person cannot always be planned ahead. At times it was necessary to make choices. This was the hard part. I actually had to think on my feet and decide at crucial moments which way the time would be distributed. Usually when such a decision was necessary, it didn't really matter because when Chester needed me it was obvious that his health and welfare always came first. However, when only "guilts" and "shoulds" faced me, then I knew those were the times I needed to care for myself.

After awhile I gained the courage to make plans with friends. I began to use my own impulses for my needs, and soon my new little social life was a normal matter of course. However, I always made sure that Chester had excellent care whether I was with him or not, and I allowed an adequate time for us to spend together as well.

Again, the key component for this new-found freedom was either having a capable live-in to assist me in my duties as caregiver, or to have arranged additional help, professionally or through my personal support group. I had to feel that I could leave my home and know I left Chester safely, in good hands. Without this feeling my life could not have progressed, for it allowed me to have the mental freedom I needed, knowing that Chester would receive good care while I was absent. And I was always careful to see that I was just a telephone call or beeper sound away in case of an emergency.

The plan fell into place on its own. There was no great deliberation or premeditation. It simply started to work. What's more, as the rhythm picked up we began to coexist in a peaceful manner. Chester was as content as he could be with his life, and I was also satisfied with the idea that maybe, just maybe, the next dance would be mine.

# 12

## A New Step

### Communication with Your Care Person

Twelve Thanksgiving tables had been set, sat at, and cleared since the doctor diagnosed Chester as having Parkinson's disease. We had reached a critical juncture. I was forced either to continue down the bleak road of loneliness, or out of repugnance to that desolate trail, reshape the path of my life using my new, healthy desires. I began to feel the hint of some tangible value causing me to arrive at this crucial breaking point. Coincidentally, Chester's daily welfare at this same time was in the hands of professional help, making the solution closer at hand.

Aware of the discoveries that I had made, I recognized the necessity for reinforcing an honest rapport with Chester. It was critical that he understand his part in the process for our common survival. I knew we had to operate as a team. Even though we had discussed our problems and their solutions before, I felt the need to leave no stone unturned. There could be no question nor doubt in either of our minds. I vividly recalled our candid discussions in the past. Our talks were always quiet, his responses usually the same. But this one time he appeared different. He seemed to know something special was about to happen.

"I need to talk to you, darling," I said cautiously. I put his hands in mine and felt his fingers tremor. His eyes stared straight into mine as he waited for me to speak. I sensed his fear, but I went on anyway. "Chester, we've got to have courage for each other. I need you on my side, sweetheart."

He listened, and nodded. "What else?" he said, as if he had expected something worse. He appeared relieved. He sighed deeply. Chester wanted my best welfare, too, as I did for him, and our knowing that about each other was essential. I couldn't talk to him so openly if I wasn't sure of that.

"We'll make it if we stick up for each other. I need to know that you'll understand that sometimes I have to have some time for myself." How could I be so selfish? I thought. I hated my words at that moment—they cut my heart into ribbons. But I knew they must be said, and they had to be received with the loving spirit that I felt. We were in this together. It seemed as if this was just one of the mysteries in life for which there was no perfect answer.

We knew our lives had crossed a threshold into new territory.

Though the Parkinson's disease had attacked his facial muscles, I could see sadness beyond his waxy expression. He took a deep breath and whispered, "I told you before, honey, don't miss anything. Live."

I clutched his hands tighter. "You'll never be out of my life, Chester. I'll never leave you behind," I said.

We trusted each other. He nodded again, as if to say, "Okay."

That was the deepest level of mutual devotion that two people could have. We felt the united spirit of our souls as if we truly were "one" at that moment. We absolutely wanted the best for each other and each of us knew it.

Even though we had similar conversations before, this one was necessary because it seemed to close out any doubt between us. It was clear that Chester never would be out of my life, nor would I ever consider him left behind. No matter what my personal needs were, they could not diminish the fact that I was proudly a married woman and intended to stay that way.

Eventually I began to feel somewhat comfortable in lengthening the periods I spent away from home. First it was a four-hour golf game; then

I stretched it out to include lunch. Soon it was dinner and either a movie or a lecture or class in which I was interested. Occasionally, I gathered my courage and went away for a couple of days by myself or with friends. I slowly became accustomed to my new lifestyle, as did Chester.

The first time I ran into old friends while I was at the theater I groped clumsily for words. I still felt embarrassed that I was out on my own, having a good time, and made unnecessary excuses for my not being home attending to Chester.

I blurted out to them, "Chester's home with the nurse. He's fine." Though they hadn't asked, I clumsily babbled on anyway hoping I would see approval written somewhere on their faces. "I'm with some old friends. I love the theater."

"Glad to see you out. Give our best to Chester," they replied. Oddly enough, they most likely were happy to see me enjoying myself, but the guilt overtook me.

At times such as these it was necessary to keep my mind's eye gazing inward and to calculate the joys the world could offer once I was able to see them. I had to look beyond the raised eyebrows that belonged to the few judgmental people, who weren't really interested in my welfare at all. I had to separate thoughts having to do with my own comfortable behavior and those regarding what I thought other people might be imagining. Many of my fears actually stemmed from fantasies of what I thought onlookers may have been thinking, but the actual reality was that the life I had begun to lead was fully supported by those very people over whom I worried. I had the courage of my convictions, and I'm sure that I chose the right road, for it ultimately led me to a happier place.

As time progressed, when I was out in public and happened to meet old friends, I felt pleased for having had the guts to maintain my life while overcoming great obstacles. Though not looking for laurels of any kind, I felt greatly rewarded by grasping what satisfying moments I could, as my happiness and contentment were accomplishments in which I took pride. I learned that life was there to enjoy, but if I didn't seize the opportunities for happiness that were presented, then I failed in my chance to live life the way it was meant to be experienced. The greatest failure was not to try. As in breaking any other barrier, the enjoyment is more remarkable when one has to fight for what is accomplished. That explains the smile that was so often on my face. I felt as if I was blessed with the good fortune of being able to dance to the same music twice.

About the time I began to look out at the world around me and flirt with the idea of taking some emotional risks, an opportunity occurred for me. Though it may seem inconsequential, at that particular time in my emotional recovery it was very important. I decided to go on a funfilled, sightseeing trip to New York City with a small band of ladies from our home community in Palm Desert, California. It was a conservative group from our local theater, and it appeared to be safe. Even though I had been to New York with Chester, this experience was different. I would be alone, and it was the first time since Chester became ill that I would leave him for more than a couple of days. In fact we were to be gone for a whole week. I'm not really sure if the excitement I felt was for the trip itself, or that I was consciously honoring some of my own personal desires. It didn't matter. What was of great consequence was my positive and happy reactions to the trip.

I prepared Chester and his nurse for my departure the best that I could and set aside in my mind whatever guilt I still had. The tour group joined together and took off to enjoy the "Big Apple" in the glory of a perfect springtime. We saw the sights of the city during the day and felt the special vibrations of New York after dark. We walked up and down Fifth Avenue in the sunshine, investigating every nook and cranny of that wonderful city, not stopping until we physically couldn't take one more step. And when the shadows of the skyscrapers cast their magical spell on New York's wondrous and famous skyline, we were right there to begin the evening's frolic. We heard the city's nightly roar, saw the bright colors of the flickering lights bounce off the marquees, and felt the intense excitement as we celebrated the nights. We stayed up until the street's hustle and bustle had gone to sleep, and we talked and laughed much of the night until our throats were pleasantly sore. For the first time in many years I felt the vitality I was sure that I was meant to feel as I was transported to a wonderful, new emotional level. It was more than a sightseeing trip with a group of ladies. It was the point at which I felt I turned my life around as if it were a mechanical object. My feelings were so elevated as I returned home on the airplane, I felt I could soar high beyond the clouds myself using only my happy emotions for wings.

At last I found my own road to recovery and knew that I reached the turning point in my journey. I was sure I had returned to living life once more. The stimulation for life grew, and I became aware that this new part of my spirit had begun. Suddenly, living took on a new meaning for me. I felt an unstoppable urge to continue to experiment in life in its more complete form.

After digesting that overwhelming, wonderful experience of traveling alone, my confidence began to build enough to give me the nerve to investigate a part of life that I had almost forgotten existed. Happiness did not fall in my lap. I worked hard to discover joys, taking emotional risks in new situations.

Stocked with these new feelings, I realized that besides my dear female friends, I also needed companions of the opposite sex to keep me company. Acknowledging these needs, this next phase of my existence became fun and exciting—a part I am glad I did not miss. I made friends with gentlemen whose company I enjoyed, and I delighted in having a pal once in awhile. I sometimes found a partner to join me in tennis and golf, and how nice it was to sit in a theater and share a concert or movie with someone beside me. It was fun to go sightseeing again with a friend, and I simply enjoyed talking to a person with a male's point of view. I thrilled each time my chair was pushed in to a table at dinner, or when I was helped on with my coat when I went outside. These molehills became mountains when I felt cared for. Little things meant a lot. And, of course, I felt happiest when the music started 'cause I knew I'd feel the slats of the dance floor beneath my feet and *I would be asked to dance*.

I never put myself in precarious situations or ever thought of walking off into the sunset with anyone. I was basically looking only for a friend, companion, or buddy. As a result of these honest and innocent motives, I found that many men, young and old, also were looking for an uncomplicated friendship. I realized how much more important these needs were for me than they were before Chester became ill. Perhaps, as the years go by, we need more nurturing and reassurance that we are appreciated in ways not necessary in more youthful and spirited years. When younger, I felt there was never going to be an end to the excitement and love in my life. At the same time, I felt in a hurry to get it all, and certain that I would. Later, I simply felt the importance of not letting a rich and beautiful segment of my life pass me by. And how much more precious it all seemed to be, having lost this pleasure for so long.

The beauties of life were waiting for me. I listened carefully to the music in my life, realized that each melody would be played only one time, and when I heard the first notes of the melody, I headed right toward the dance floor.

# 13

## A Texas Two-Step

### Courage Replaces Fear

I entered this next part of my life with a more measured calm. Panic and crises disappeared, making it possible to move on to a new, healthier kind of happiness—one born from finding the courage to explore my ideals and to shape my dreams out of the valuable experiences and faith I encountered along the way.

I learned to speak up when faced with intimidation and learned to remain quiet when I wanted to scream from frustration. I learned to take risks when I couldn't be sure of the results, while closing my eyes to the stark tragedies I faced. I laughed when I wanted to cry, and held someone else tightly when they were sad. I reached out for help when my heart was breaking, and gained humility when I asked a friend to wipe my tears because the pain was too great to bear alone. I learned to admit my mistakes when I was wrong, and to support my beliefs when I thought I was right. I stood up to the world when my life style became different, and when they said, "No you can't," I replied, "Why not?" And while my outward appearance improved, I knew the face I saw in my mirror had changed only because a happier soul lived within me.

Eventually, I learned to act upon healthy physical or emotional desires and was able to rearrange my life to produce a more satisfying existence. I addressed every situation separately and made the effort to insure its success without disturbing other parts of life that could not be comfortably altered. I calculated the moves in my life as if I were a Grand Master of chess, moving the chess men to squares that allowed me to control the board. Although the results were not always what I wanted, most of the time I was on target. Many times I didn't always know where my queen would end up, but I felt certain that the pawns would be gone before the game was over. The long-term results were not always what I expected, but the shorter goals were most often satisfying experiences.

For me, the key to feeling better was to explore all possibilities regardless of their magnitude. I found that I couldn't put pleasure in a cup and decide how much of it to pour out at a particular time. I was perceptive enough to know when blessings were being offered to me and to accept them when they appeared. Some of my most memorable experiences lasted only a few minutes, but there wasn't a scale large enough to weigh their value. What a pity it would have been to have missed these simple joys of life, merely because I hoped for a grander occurrence down the road.

A moment of complete happiness came one morning when I was awakened by the delicate notes of Mozart's music playing on my little radio beside my bed. As the bright rays of sunshine began to fill my window, the mockingbird's first sounds mingled with the delicate melody of the lovely sonata. There I met a peace which could not be measured. And as our lives together progressed, Chester and I sometimes laughed a little while sharing intimate thoughts as we lingered over a cup of tea. And I knew that for moments such as these, that's all there was, and it was enough. Sometimes the truly little things had the ingredients that produced the most happiness in my life. If I added a little enjoyment to the average day, then I was successful for those twenty-four hours. That's what it was all about for me in those years of studying the important lessons of life.

Victories were made possible by my looking beyond the fears that could have stopped me if I had let them. Anxieties could have easily restricted or blocked my fruitful accomplishments. Like guilt, fear became a painful and useless emotion. However, fear, like guilt, subsided and eventually lost its power to sabotage the development of positive elements in my world.

Just as it took strength to rebuild the framework of my life, I required a new kind of vitality to move into a more relaxed state of mind. Though I had traveled through difficult and seemingly impossible times, all the while the fearful situations I encountered were familiar. I dealt with my past traumas and worked through them to solutions, moving across well-known territories. But as I trudged the road to new horizons, softer and quieter though it seemed, it was a new and unfamiliar road and once more I had to look beyond the fear that greeted me.

Most of the poor decisions I made could be directly related to the tangible quality of fear itself. Thus, I began to label fear a "happiness blocker" and tried to determine if fear lay behind any of my life choices. If in any way I felt as if it would deter me from proceeding in a planned course of action, then I took a deep breath and said, "Go." Or if I started any sentence with "I'm afraid of...," then I would rethink my plan and more than likely take the chance. Once I found this magic formula to keep me from falling into fear's trap, I was able to get to the other side of my problems and enjoy the dreams about which I fantasized for so long. If fear could come between me and pleasure, I fought it. If I had a choice between basking in the joys of pleasure or wallowing in the abyss of fear, then I'd go for pleasure every time.

After many years of giving up sleep that was rightly mine, I finally stopped the all-night or early-morning conferences in my brain. I learned how to look at my problems and see them not as problems at all, but as situations with alternatives. It worked!

Next, I had to take responsibility for acting like a grown-up. Remaining in a private and safe world, like a turtle withdrawn into his shell, is not a valid method for attaining self-realization and becoming a fully actualized human being. On the contrary, my self-esteem grew the more courageous I became, and those around me respected me more when I outwardly asserted my own needs. When I saw that certain conditions in my life were immutable, I was forced to change only what was possible—myself.

Finally I redefined the concept of respectability. To feel good about myself, I had to have peace and harmony in my life. I couldn't have self-respect and at the same time be resentful for not having the life I desired. Nor could I expect anyone else to respect me if I could not respect myself. Respectability began with a new confidence. It made my eyes continue to shine when all the apparent debits on the balance sheet of my life far exceeded the assets. When I felt the rich glow of self-esteem, even though the calculations hadn't changed, the world was baffled when I came out ahead with my emotional bank brimming over.

I recall vividly how scared I was in the beginning to take even the smallest actions to add to my new life experiences. I quivered with fear when I ventured away from what was tried, true, and familiar. My worries felt the same, whether wondering if I could keep up with my peers in a computer or economics class, or even participating in a sports activity that I loved.

I'll never forget the first time I went Western dancing. I stood by myself in a corner of the small Western night club listening to boots scooting across the dance floor while I watched the dancers in each other's arms, wending their way around the floor, keeping time to the infectious rhythm. I felt frightened…afraid of being asked to dance, and at the same time feeling afraid of not being asked. Though it may seem a small and insignificant incident on the caregiver's scale of life, later that night when a lovely Western ballad poured from the sound system at the Cactus Corral, absolutely nothing was more important to me than when a handsome cowboy removed the twin-edged fear. He came face-to-face with me, tipped his big black Western hat, and asked with a soft Texas drawl, "Would you like to do a Texas two-step with me, ma'am?"

I took a deep breath, "Yes I would. I sure would," I said bravely. I tried to cover up my nervousness, held out my hand, and before I knew it I was only concentrating on "Quick, quick, slow, slow, quick, quick, slow…"

The important thing is that I did not allow fear to dominate my desires. When I continued straight ahead in a "no matter what" direction, whatever I had feared most became my friend. As with so many of the tools that I learned to use through the years, my success rate went up commensurately with the total number of new experiences I undertook.

Once I walked through a fear, I never had that same one again, and instead of feeling its frightening effects, I grew confident knowing that I could handle the next challenge.

Though this attitude may seem self-serving, as I continued to enjoy my hard-won, positive feelings, I found that my peace of mind made me feel more comfortable with what I naturally did for others. Though the job of a caregiver was not easy, the happier and more content I became with my own life, the more quality I added to Chester's. If I was happy, then my good feelings were transferred to Chester, and ultimately returned to me again.

Life as a caregiver was far from perfect, but it was my reality. Even though I knew that I could not make a faultless world for myself or the others that were involved, I had the responsibility to give it my best efforts. The accountability to myself, Chester, and the rest of our families was linked to building my own happiness.

While occasionally I took a break from my daily routine, perhaps even from my total environment, I always remained a caregiver. I never really left Chester's side, nor did the overall responsibilities and duties built into my life ever cease to exist. I was either thinking or planning (usually ahead), but always fully absorbed, and my job never stopped. In my role as caregiver, a deep, frightening reality spoke to me all the time and I knew that I must make it work as well as a fallible human being could.

The nature of living is such that everyone is faced with his own kinds of problems. People find the courage to withstand the devastating loss of life and property due to the destruction of wars or natural events. Families are sometimes uprooted from their homes by hurricanes, tornadoes, floods, earthquakes, fires, and other forms of havoc—and the dysfunctional family combats a disease of the soul on a daily basis. Somehow, human nature gives the victims strength to rebuild their lives once more. People pick themselves up and start over again—and again, and again. So did I, as caregiver. Every day.

Once one knows the bitter taste of sadness and disappointment one can also more easily smell the sweetest, subtlest scent of flowers when they blossom. As the sun sets at twilight, the rays are a little more golden, and the sky shines with a few extra twinkling stars when nighttime sets in for those who have traveled the low roads of sorrow and tragedy.

I am asked why I appeared so happy during this troubled period of my life. My only answer is that I tried not to miss one of those golden sunsets as I built up a store of light within. As one's situation changes, so does the yardstick by which one measures his own lifetime. For Chester, the greatest quality of all was his ability to hang onto every last remnant of his life. And for me, the height of my greatest rewards was simply to watch my husband take just one more step. That was the worthwhile existential quality to which I clung that could not be measured. The quality of our lives actually was enhanced by the limitations we had to endure.

One of the most treasured moments in my life occurred on Valentine's Day in 1994, fifteen years from the beginning of it all. By this time Chester could barely speak and he could not move from place to place without assistance, confined only to his wheelchair or bed. His mental state was fragile and communication was most often nil. So what was I to think when the doorbell rang and I saw a delivery boy holding a beautiful bouquet of long-stem red roses, apparently a Valentine for somebody. I quickly said to the young man, "Judy lives next door. You've made a mistake." But how I secretly wished they were for me. I started to close the door and wished I had never seen the bright red, gorgeous bouquet.

"No, Miss, these flowers were sent by your husband." The young man smiled, "See here," and he pointed to the card that simply said, "I love you, Chester."

That loving act had the strength to move mountains and was laden with all of the precious jewels in the world. An unforgettable, treasured moment in my life that I surely would never forget.

Because of experiencing times of such majestic significance, my feet became planted firmly on the ground and, understanding the direction of my life, I was able to leap above the daily problems I had to face. At a time when the most fearful dismantling of my lifestyle was taking place, I found that I could avoid the collapse of my emotional state along with it. When I heard the clinking of Chester's walker or his wheelchair rolling along our hallway's floor, instead of feeling heartbreak and fear, I somehow awakened to the fact that he was fit enough to be with me one more day. When we sat together and visited I felt joy in knowing that we had another conversation, even though mine was the only audible voice. When we spoke to one another, I knew what he was saying by reading the thoughts in his expressive green eyes, and I spoke to him as if his responses were uttered vocally. Instead of lamenting the incapacity his terrible illness produced, and dwelling on the fact that he could hardly speak, I clung to the subdued happiness that our spiritual rapport brought us.

I am grateful for knowing that our marriage retained a special beauty and warmth even though we were forced to travel the long road of tragedy. When I recall my husband's masculine spirit and handsome strength before his illness began, I comprehend the relation of his determination to continue uprightly in his final years. My evaluation of our lives allows me to understand my part in this mysterious dance of life and know that I have indeed been enriched by learning to give of myself and serve another human being emotionally and spiritually.

At times it seemed impossible to go on, but I did anyway. And as I look back at this most difficult period in my life, I find joy in my heart. I realized that I had been given the opportunity to be by my husband's side, physically, emotionally, and spiritually, in the most critical time of his life. Not many people are so gifted—to be the only person another human being depends on, literally, for life's every need. Yes, it seems like a huge responsibility—and so it was. But great rewards only come with enormous sacrifice and dedication. So caregivers, if you're ever feeling exploited to the maximum and you feel as if you're going to burst, remember this reward shall remain in your heart. The fact here is that you were chosen, and that in itself is your gift.

It is true that to survive as a moderately happy person through my career as caregiver I had to build a life for myself outside the immediate sphere of the infirmed environment. However, the most memorable and precious experiences I had in my life were in the last fourteen years with my husband, and no one could judge the quality of our lives from the outside. When others saw Chester slumped in his wheelchair with me by his side, my arms clasped around his shoulder, what could they know of the ingredients of our satisfying moments? Everyone's dance is different.

Thanksgiving 1993 arrived, and the autumn tones once more cast their golden hue upon us. Fourteen times we had watched the seasons change since we were first taken hostage by my husband's illness. Our entire family reunited again around the dinner table this particular Thanksgiving holiday. We all knew it was special, and we were grateful to have one more time for us all to be together. More places were set around the table than were there fourteen years before, as we enjoyed the additional joy of grandchildren and a new niece and nephew. When I carved the turkey on Thanksgiving Day, I watched the reflection of the desert sun tease the flames on the candles that stood proudly in the carved candlesticks that Chester and I bought on our honeymoon twenty-nine years before. The melody that played in the background of this tranquil scene was a song of gratitude and freedom. The hostages were free at last.

The time had come to approach the last dance enthusiastically, enter unfamiliar areas of life, and shed the fear and guilt which stiffened my movements in the past. I hoped that I had the courage and strength to answer life's difficult calls with the grace of the little dancing ballerina that delicately spins and twirls in precise beautiful movements atop a child's music box. There is only one performance here on earth, and it must be done without a dress rehearsal, one dance at a time.

# 14

## Save the Last Dance for Me

### Acceptance

But I Can Still Dance continued for me past the last pages of this book, but Chester's part of the story ended when he crossed the threshold of a nursing home to spend the closing days of his life receiving total care. This part of our lives, after thirty years of marriage, finally took us in separate directions. When absolutely all other options were exhausted, though we never spiritually were separated, we acceded at last to parting from each other.

After his doctor told us that Chester needed to make a move to a nursing facility, we sat down one day with a close cousin of Chester and discussed the few alternatives left for us and what would ultimately be best for him.

Nate put his arm around Chester's shoulder. Tenderly, he said, "Ches, the doctor says it's time for you to start living in a place where you can be cared for all the time. You need more attention now. He's afraid you'll break some bones falling if you don't." There was complete silence. Then Chester looked at me, and with a strained voice barely above a whisper said, "Honey, we better give it a shot." That was one of the last rational, and audible, sentences he would ever speak. Chester was ready. He couldn't fight the illness anymore, and he knew it.

Strangely, as he made the decision regarding the last days of his life, his final choice also pointed me along a different route. Though I agonized many sleepless nights with the decision of whether or not to place Chester in the health care facility, I am certain the transition for me was easier because of the life that I created for myself in a separate, healthy and loving environment during the time preceding his move. The positive lessons I learned in the last years of Chester's illness were specifically born from the experiences I encountered during this painful period. I learned to love another person selflessly, kindly, and generously; and to open my hand, my heart, and my soul, not focusing on what I would receive in return. I derived special joy watching my loved one beat the odds against his never-ending battle each time he was called to fight. With absolute certainty, I discovered that there was neither a right nor wrong way to live life. "My way," as Alice, my psychologist, said was the only way for me. It was possible, and indeed workable, to live two completely independent lives, savoring each to the fullest, enjoying the essence of both, while denying nothing to either of them.

On July 1, 1994, Chester was wheeled into the Monterey Palms Nursing Home in Palm Desert. There he continued his last days, struggling to respond to his natural and normal environment. His once strong legs became unusable, his body too weak to move from bed. At this devastating time in his life, he was reduced to being spoon fed, diapered, and treated as if he were an infant. He could not speak. However, even though his condition was frail, it was clear that he felt comfortable and safe. The passage to this next place in Chester's life appeared to be smooth for him apparently because he sensed that, as ever, he would continue to have the best care possible. The quality of care he received was in fact, excellent and it dispelled for me the idea that all nursing homes were to be feared. I'm greatly relieved that we were able to place him in a good home so that he could live his final days in comfort.

In addition, Community Hospice Care entered his existence immediately and took over many duties that private nurses had done in the past. The hospice staff was cheerful, friendly and responsible. A loving representative visited Chester several times a week to see that all of his physical and emotional needs were met. These individuals were gently supportive as well as practical and kind, and they seemed to have an extra special sensitivity to other human beings.

One day, I watched quietly as Alma, his dear hospice friend, stood by his bed, stroked his brow, and soothingly whispered, "Good morning, Chester. You're especially handsome today."

She smoothed his silvery hair glistening in the sunlight that streamed through the window. Her pleasing manner relaxed him so much that his lips showed a slight smile, and he breathed softly as she placed earphones on his head so that he could listen to the big band music he'd always cherished. He didn't need to respond in words. He was peaceful, and we knew it.

As if the generous care from Hospice for my husband were not enough, this wonderful organization assigned a special social worker to guide me in many important decisions at this time regarding Chester's death and funeral. These were trying moments, and I'm grateful that this last heavy load was made lighter due to the sound advice given to me by Sandy, my own Hospice counselor.

My loving husband, Chester Breskin, died peacefully February 3, 1995.

Having done all that I could to ease his last days, I moved on to the next phase of my own life. At the close of the last chapter of our lives together, a door remained open for the continuation of the new life I began for myself several years before. Even with the sadness surrounding us at that crucial time, I knew that my own story was not over and the last dance was saved for me.

A new focus took shape in my life resulting from the time I had for quiet contemplation and being alone. Inner changes and growth had taken place, and opportunities to find out who I am and what is important to me had come in the course of living. In a peculiar way, new areas of life that seemed impossible before became plausible.

Instead of feeling my life was finished, I felt a sense of renewed hope, and free to pursue interests that were denied me in the past. I realized that two lives do not need to end because of the tragedy of one.

I believe that my strongest needs and desires will be fulfilled because I learned the importance of contributing to the welfare of others. For me, the greatest lesson of all was to fully understand that as long as I am willing, the lessons need never cease and that the true purpose of life is to live. The gifts of living are given in strange ways that I may never understand...

The mysteries of life unfold in their own time, in their own way. A beginning, an end. Another beginning. From health to sickness—and one hopes, back to health again. The journey of life is not the sum of all the peaks, but also the hills and valleys in between. A gathering in, a letting go.

The long night finally ends with the birth of a new day. The sun, ever new, rises slowly, majestically out of the mountains to the east, sending rosy fingers into crevices among the peaks in the west. Soon the valley is bathed in magentas, pinks, oranges, and yellows. Night critters scurry to their dens. Day animals begin their search for a sustenance. Leaves uncurl, stretch, and open their surfaces to the sun's rays. Petals unfurl.

At last I open my arms and embrace the living. It is good, this life.

# PART TWO
# PRACTICAL
# LIVING

# 1

## Realizing There is a Beginning, Middle, and End to Every Problem

The struggle that began for me on the eve of Thanksgiving 1979, and what appeared to be the greatest tragedy of my life, eventually became the basis for the valuable standards of living that I developed. I am not one to love martyrdom, and of course I wish that we could have avoided this part of our lives—but the fact is that we couldn't. It was our life and had to be lived out in the manner in which it was given to us. Hard as it was, in many ways, the experience of dealing with the effects of Chester's tragic illness added a dimension to my life that resulted in immeasurable and precious gifts of the heart. Within the turmoil, confusion, and sadness for me lay instruction for the greatest art of all, "the art of living."

It has been said that difficulties are merely learning lessons. How well we learn from something that smacks us in the face, not letting up for an instant. It's ironic that we look back and only see in our rear view mirror what gifts those lessons were. For those exercises in my life stretched my inward emotional muscles and expanded my nature, allowing me to reach out later in life in the emotional assistance and giving to others in need. I learned how to be a more loving friend, grandmother, mother, daughter, and lover. I learned the real essence of intimacy and how to really care about someone more than myself. And what's more, I learned how to act on that valuable friendship. So you see, these lessons are not only for the time being, they are gifts for a lifetime.

Sixteen years later, when this precious education was completed I realized a joy and fulfillment in my life far greater than what might ever have been contemplated. And you will too. Although from time to time you will feel as if you have to deal with life's burdens, which are too much for your capability, you can and indeed will rise to it if you are aware that what you are experiencing is only a gap in life's adventures. The reward is in the richness and fulfillment that you feel when you help another person that you love, and that alone is the most powerful experience one can imagine.

I sincerely hope that the experiences and ideas that I recount here will be helpful for you to live a balanced and healthier life. You will find the strength, hope, and courage that you need at this crucial time if you remember that there is a beginning, middle, and ending to every problem.

# 2

## Surviving the First Emotional Trauma

Shock, loss, grief, and pain is the normal progression of the stages of your own part of your care person's illness. You will pull through and recover from your shock, loss, grief, and pain if you allow yourself to travel through the stages of recovery realizing that what you are going through are normal life experiences in your situation. From time to time you may feel as if you are losing control, but you will bounce back to having a feeling of normalcy without even being aware of it. Even though you may think that you can't handle the initial shock, if you remember that others have survived the same exact experiences, then you will know that you can, and will, too. Your road will be a little easier to follow knowing that other survivors have walked the same path before you. Expect it to hurt, because it will, but know that with each recovery the hurt will be replaced with a new-found courage and strength.

The depth of your sadness is appropriate for your loss, and the loss is devastating. It has to be. Besides worrying about your loved one, you're probably thinking that your life will never be the same. You're right, it won't, but that doesn't mean that you can't go on and find ways to live your new life in a satisfactory and happy manner.

Don't be afraid of the words of a diagnosis. They are just words. It is not necessary to rush through the illness, as a chronic illness can take many years to manifest itself. Stay in the "now" as much as possible and concentrate on the present time with which you must deal. Projection into the years ahead will only cause you unnecessary fears. Most of the things you will worry about won't happen anyway. Try to distinguish between real fears and the fear of fear itself.

Stay close to the person you are caring for as long as you can. Concentrate on the richness of your lives and dwell on "the haves" of your relationship, instead of the "have nots." You will be surprised as to how many more positives there are in your lives if you focus on them.

Listen carefully to what the person you are caring for has to say, and talk to one another as much as possible. Keep a constant dialogue going between you and your care person, and the channels of communication will remain open. You will be able to rely on each other now just as you have done in the past—you need each other more than ever. Hang on to your spouse physically as well as emotionally, and continue loving, physical contact for as long as possible. Make an effort to keep your sex life active, and experiment in new methods of satisfaction for one another as your care person's sexual abilities diminish. Persist in touching and holding on, and enjoy the warmth of your bodies together. This intimacy will far exceed the orgasmic thrill. It may be the greatest ammunition that you have against the symptoms of the illness, but especially at the beginning. Once you reinforce that you are able to enjoy this physical contact, you will see that it can continue and actually will not need to leave you for a long time.

Accept, if you can, as soon as you can, the grief that you can't avoid. Remember, "Denial" is a river in Egypt. Leave it there. The sooner you recognize your grief for what it is, the sooner will be your recovery. You will find that you actually can handle it. At the same time, hang onto your hopes and dreams. Acknowledge your pending future, knowing that you have one. Some of your plans are still possible, and others may remain only fantasies that are appropriate for you to think about. Enjoy them as long as they don't create disappointments for you.

Spend additional time with your family, especially grandchildren, if they are logistically close to you. If not nearby, then call them regularly. Their voices will be healing to you in times of sadness and stress.

Keep an open forum with your close friends as well. Bring them into your lives. Shorten the charade that you are living. It is natural to want to run away from your friends, but don't. You need them, and they will not understand your withdrawal. You will not diminish yourself in anyway by admitting to the people who love you that you're scared. You will only widen the trust and love between you.

Appreciate the fact that the cold icy feeling in your bones and the sick pit in your stomach are symptoms of grief that will subside. Don't be discouraged if they return, as they will from time to time. The losses will be new and recurring, but the dismissal process will remain the same—over and over again. Grief and loss must take their normal course. However there are bereavement and loss support groups that can help you move through this process. Call a hospital, Synagogue or Church in your area and request a support care group for grief and loss.

If you are undergoing the shock surrounding the illness of a parent or other close family member or friend, allow yourself the necessary time to grieve the extreme loss of the significant part in your life that the person played. Besides feeling pain for someone that you love, the loss of a strong parental or supportive and authoritative figure can be especially excruciating if one has been accustomed to their emotional brace for many years. Acceptance here may be the hardest feat you may ever have to endure. It is so very difficult to watch a role model revert from the strong figure you always looked up to and admired to a parent with diminishing physical and mental faculties. But if you know that you must intellectually accept this fact, then you can and will, and your own vital assistance will be more valuable.

Though you may feel that the music in your life has come to a sudden stop, understand that a different sort of melody is just beginning to play. You will learn the dances that go with the music, just as in learning any other dance. It will be new and unfamiliar at first, but once you have caught on, you will feel the rhythm again and you will continue dancing through life.

Miraculous as it may seem, you can live this stage of your life fearlessly as a happy, accepting, self-actualized person. You can be content with today, and although you may wish yesterday could have been different, you need not be afraid of tomorrow.

# 3

# *Understanding Your Shame*

Being ashamed of the illness can be brought into a healthy perspective when you accept the situation as it is. You are neither better nor worse than anyone who is not a caregiver. Many people are sick, and many people are well. It is not a crime, nor is it antisocial behavior to be sick. The pity lies in the fact of one's withdrawal when someone is ill, when actually support is then needed from your friends and family the most. Don't feel ashamed for losing the part of your life that was seized from you. It is not your fault.

It is often common to hide the fact that your loved one has contracted a dreaded chronic illness at the onset of a major ailment. But if you are open and honest at the start, there will be one less obstacle for you to overcome. Going straight at it with your friends will shorten your unnecessary embarrassment. Remember, "The shortest distance between two points is a straight line."

It's a natural feeling to want to run away, but the sooner you admit your needs, the sooner they will be answered. It's hard to climb walls, so don't build them between you and the people you need in your life. Share your crises with those who love you. You're not really alone unless you choose to have it so. The more you look beyond your feeling different, the less importance any difference will have.

The dreadful misfortune of illness is its quality of being uncontrollable, and it can happen to anyone. There are no rewards for controlling illness, and lack of control is a part of life. Just when you think you have a hold on life, the circumstances change anyway, so don't waste time worrying about the lack of control. Know that there will be changes down the line because the fact is that the only thing constant in life is change, and you simply cannot change that.

Go to your friends and explain in detail the issues you are encountering and just how your lives are being affected. You will find that once it is out in the open, the impact will lessen. You may not be as different as you think. You're more conscious of the circumstances than anyone else. As your limitations cause you to alter your life, try to adjust to the tempo in which you need to live, but live within that realm for as long as possible. Don't give away all of your expectations, hopes, and dreams with your care person. Some will never go away, and some may take many years to dwindle. Most important of all, don't give away any of your own hopes and dreams while you are still capable of living a fruitful life.

Changes will likely occur in the life of one with a chronic illness, but make a point to continue to enjoy as much life as possible outside your home with your care person, doing normal activities for as long as you can. You will feel less self-conscious the more you and your care person participate in public life. Make every effort to attend events and functions you enjoy. Don't give up your evenings out to the theater and concerts. Make music a significant part of your lives—as it is immensely soothing. It will relax and enrich each of you, and both of you together.

Naturally, you want your loved one back the way he or she was before the illness took over—but that is impossible. If you are embarrassed by them in any way, don't beat yourself up for having these feelings. You're not the first caregiver in the world to feel that way. What you are feeling has nothing to do with the quality of love you have for the person in your care. In fact, it is possible that you are feeling the embarrassment for your loved one because you know that what the world sees now is not the real person within him. Besides which, your strong love for your beloved is probably what makes you want to protect his feelings even more. Your own self-worth has also been attacked, and once your confidence starts to be rebuilt then you will feel more comfortable in general.

It's okay to admit that you want a normal life. Everyone does. However, a new life for you as a caregiver has been created. And for you, that is your normal life. Watch for the point in time when you can give up the inner struggle and take a step to the side. Once you reach that point, be happy to admit that you are capable of a full life. It is your responsibility to your care person, yourself, and to life in general to live proudly for as long as you have your own good health. Self-survival is not selfish. It merely "is." Martyrdom is what is selfish, and it is no fun at all. Your care person has enough problems. Don't lay a heap of guilt on him as well. They are doing the best that they can, and allow them the dignity they deserve.

Seek help from a professional—either a psychologist, psychiatrist, clergy, or a support group affiliated with your care person's illness. There is a support group for most illnesses in every major city. You need to speak with those with whom you can be thoroughly honest and will really understand your feelings.

You can have a satisfying life even though the dances may be slower. Live your dreams while you have them. See every sunrise and sunset that you can with your loved one, and grasp every potential bit of happiness together. These moments may be the most precious ones you've yet enjoyed because now their value has increased!

Don't worry about wanting a life of your own. It will be there for you when you decide you are ready for it.

Be proud of yourself for the job you are doing. The task is a tough one. So, pat yourself on the back for your efforts. Hold your head high, and be good to yourself. You deserve it.

# 4

## Accepting Your New Role in Life

Living in a couple's world is a new realization for you. You will find in it a unique and different feeling than you felt before. But what you are feeling, is simply a change to which you can adapt. You may not feel like "one of the group" with your old friends anymore, because though sad as the situation is, you may not be. Your social situation needs a good, strong reevaluation. One solution may be that you might now need to seek some new companions for you and your spouse for awhile. "There are more ways than one to skin a cat." And this cat has a lot of coats. So don't give in to the feeling that you are falling into a deep hole, and you will from now on be alone. That is not true—all is not lost. You must now stick with "the winners" for you and your mate, and the "winner's circle" is just a step to the side.

Learn the difference and distinguish between devotee and casual friends. You may enjoy the fun with the casuals, but the devotees will ultimately end up saving your souls. Decide how important it really is to get out with casual friends before you subject yourselves to undue and unnecessary humiliation and rejection. The time is over for "slick, hip, and cool." All at once, those "one-liners" are not so funny anymore. Instead, as you make new friends you will find them to have a deeper quality of warmth and sincerity than did your old acquaintances. If they are of the ilk to be sensitive to your problems and want to socialize with you and your care person, they are truly the kind of friends that you want and need in your life right now. People like this do exist. A few loyal and trustworthy friends are far more important than all of the social events in the world. Nor do you need a large group of people to protect you from loneliness, either. One or two couples with a loving nature is more than enough to carry you through this next period.

If and when you sense a pulling back from your old friends, or see uneasy expressions on their faces, go to a confidant and hope you will receive some honest answers so that you can be sure of your feelings. This is no time for guessing games, as your emotional stability and inner feelings are at stake. There is nothing worse than experiencing mixed messages. Though the reply may hurt at the beginning, the candid voice may be just what you need to get you set for your new beginning. You will undoubtedly thank the truthful person, as you will at least know what to expect. If you feel as if you are "hitting your emotional bottom" and cannot take one more subtle rejection, remember that you are on the right track and your pain will ultimately lead you out of your loneliness to a more pleasant place. This is what it might take to force you to understand the complicated yet simple problem. At that point, and as the time progresses, you will see that you will eventually be ready to find some happiness on your own and still continue to stay close physically and socially to your spouse.

Keep your eyes on the real issues and not on your sensitivities. If you're hurt, don't apologize for your feelings. It's okay to hurt. A great deal has been removed from your life in just the thought that you may have lost the companion on your life's adventures. Try to understand it is not you or your care person who is being rejected. It is the situation, and you can be assured, "they" do not mean to hurt you, "they" simply cannot help it now.

Most importantly, "high class problems" of a social nature are still problems, and they can be the most difficult to solve since they are complicated and infiltrated by, and with, guilt. They also hurt just as much as problems of seemingly more magnitude. Given both to solve, I bet I solve the bigger ones faster, and with more finesse, than the smaller ones. I bet you do, too. Don't sweep them under the carpet and pretend they don't exist. They do, and they need to be addressed.

Talk to a psychologist or counselor. If one is not readily available, then seek assistance from a rabbi, priest, or clergy. The problem can be solved, and is not one that should be "stuffed down" or repressed. Being "left out" is not minor if it hurts you. The problem can be solved if you accept the reality as it unfolds. However, you will find it difficult, if not impossible, to survive this quandary if you try to make it as a "married-single" in a couple's world where "it takes two to tango."

# 5

## *Exercise Your Freedom*

Freedom is precious. Don't waste it. It is yours for the taking, so take it! Recognize your options, choices and the value of freedom. It is the one thing you must never take for granted because every part of your life depends on it. Freedom is the bedrock from which your dreams can be built, and your dreams can become your reality if you explore your freedom. With both freedom and your new reality built from your dreams, you have a chance to do whatever you choose.

Once you begin to exercise your options, you will see that you have many, and your productivity will bring you new unexpected pleasures. Then, as your enjoyment builds, you will find that the guilt that you may have worried about, need not exist at all.

Realize and fully understand that you are powerless as far as your care person's health is concerned. There is no way for you to make him well, but don't let him make you sick, either. Examine both of your needs and be sure to respond to your own. Give yourself the strokes you crave, throwing in some luxuries that will produce extra joy and happiness for you. Someday you may be incapacitated yourself, so enjoy your life while you can. There is certainly great sadness surrounding a chronic illness, however, the greatest tragedy of all is to give up the freedom of your own life when it is not necessary, and especially while you are still healthy. Value your own healthy life as well as your own freedom. You're so lucky to have them both. Life goes by a lot quicker when you are in good health.

Just because your care person is sick, don't fall into the trap of allowing him to run your entire life. "Come out of the closet" with your needs and reevaluate the restrictions that have been controlling you. This time don't be afraid to start your sentence with "I need..." As your spirit is set free, you can release yourself from the previous strict boundaries that controlled your thoughts. With a little practice, you will find that you can be passively assertive without injuring anybody, and this approach will benefit everybody involved.

Your new life will be enjoyable and can even be more fun than it ever was before. Don't let the good things intimidate you. Be aware of opportunities that will suddenly appear in your life, and remember it is all part of your new freedom. Go for them! Enjoy the cultivation of new friendships, and cast away old ideas of restricted values. Concentrate on the spiritual value, as well as the traditional and eccentric in the nature of your new companions. Be selective in your new collection of personalities, but be sure not to waste time on "nonsense." You now have the time to "pick and choose."

If you make a mistake, so what?—you have the time to recoup. Don't be afraid to lose, and you just might find yourself a winner if you are brave enough to take the emotional risk. Remember, the only sin is not to try. Time is not the issue now; the present is all that is important. Don't worry about the future. If unpleasant changes are to occur in your care person's life, they will happen soon enough, and they probably will take their place in your lives at a digestible pace. Worrying about them in advance will not head them off, so let them go if you can.

Grab your second chance in life, and be grateful it is yours. It's not everyone that has a "second time around the daisies." Learn and appreciate the distinction between what really is valuable and what is not. Begin with "what is," and concentrate on the value of your own life. As you answer your own true needs, do what you desire to create your new pleasures—of course being sure not to jeopardize your care person's welfare in any way. Find ways to mobilize your own dreams, and coincidentally, a new and deeper love, respect and appreciation will automatically flow between you and your care person. Remember, your care person will ultimately be the benefactor of your improved mental and physical health.

Kick up your heels once in a while, and have some fun. Don't look for the "pot of gold at the end of the rainbow." Remember that "the richest rewards are sprinkled along the way of the journey."

# 6

## *The Solutions Begin*

The real solutions will begin when you admit that you are part of a family illness. After you recognize your role in the situation it will be easier to assess the circumstances more objectively. Be willing to stop hiding behind the illness and face up to your own needs. The only way they will ever be met is if you recognize that your needs do exist. The ability to enjoy life begins with the responsibility to live without blaming your unhappiness on the illness. The longer you run from the reality, the more you will believe that it is true; and conversely, the less power you give it, the less strength it will have over you.

The only rewards for "Over-caregiver of the Year" are over-work, over-strain, and over-stress. When the prize is presented, make sure you're not the winner. Start your self-healing process by taking actions to ease your pain with some self-respect, self-love, and self-tenderness. Much more worthwhile awards! F. Scott Fitzgerald said, "Show me a hero and I'll show you a tragedy." You may not be able to alter the course of your dear one's tragedy, but you don't have to jump in beside him and play hero if it will only hurt you both.

Create an imaginary visual image for yourself which represents you. For instance, whenever you're frightened, close your eyes and imagine a baby that needs your care. Picture yourself as that helpless soul and in your mind watch yourself nurture that wee child. Cuddle it, stroke it, love it. The positive energy of this mantra held in your thoughts for a few minutes will give you strength to surmount the challenge that you are facing and will hold you steady until you are back on the right track. You will find that you can walk through fear instead of retreating. Before you say "I'm sorry, I can't," think of the words "I can," and then decide if you indeed can and want to do what is asked of you. Push yourself that extra little bit. Chances are you'll make it, and you will feel much better when you do.

Begin to consider constructive ideas and new methods for obtaining your happy life. They will be exciting as they will be your very own creations. Allow yourself the privilege of finding new strengths that have lain dormant within you for so long. You will see that once you take a risk, the next formidable task will be easier to start, and soon you will create a new pattern of living with unrestrained values.

Grasp at opportunities as they appear. The accomplishment of adding new interests to your life not only will be fun, but will lead you on to the next phase and interest that presents itself. Listen and watch for little things that interest you. The small experiences will be easier for you at the beginning, then later, get involved with larger commitments.

Be proud of the new brand of courage you are developing while still being a loving caregiver. Have the courage to make choices, with you as the benefactor of the decisions. If you falter or make a mistake, get right back on course and continue once more with new choices. Choice is the key to your emotional freedom, and positive choices will bring you there faster. Re-prioritize!

Find the courage to go "out there" alone and recognize yourself as an individual. Do the things in life that you always thought about and didn't have the time, inclination, nor courage to pursue. At the beginning, take "baby steps." Go slowly, but go. Venture beyond the curtains in your living room and join the life that is waiting for you. You will be greeted with happy surprises. Make games of and enjoy your new challenges.

Mingle, and make new friendships. Find some new playmates and have some fun! It will relieve some of your loneliness. Face up to the fact that you are an adult with well-deserved desires for companions and friends. Your refreshment and revitalization will make you a happier person, improve the morale of your care person, and improve the general vibrations and vitality in your home. Don't be embarrassed by wanting to have some enjoyment in life. Even though your care person will ultimately benefit by a "happier you," the one who will really benefit will actually be you.

Enjoy your new found pleasures—you don't need to feel guilty about being happy. After feeling as if the weight of the world has been on your shoulders for so long, relish your new relief. Recognize guilt for what it is—a useless element. Walk through it. Don't stop to visit with guilt, nor waste any valuable time with it, and it won't hurt you. Don't authenticate it; remove the word "guilt" from your vocabulary, and you will truly believe that it doesn't exist. Replace your negative addictions to guilt, depression, and sadness with positive factors, including your fresh or renewed friendships and interests. The new elements will be more powerful than your previous negative habits, and they will instill joy in your life. You will then see how easy it is to eliminate guilt and other negative factors with pleasure.

Most important, find the courage to go "out there" with your spouse (or care person) and take risks among society, together. This may help you to have confidence when you go out there alone. Not only will your care person appreciate getting out, but you will enjoy the feeling of giving him one more pleasant afternoon or evening. Try a movie, or go for a walk with your careperson in the wheelchair. Go out for an ice cream cone or a cappuccino at the local coffee shop. Venture out to the mall and go shopping, or spend an afternoon at the library together. Do normal things and you will feel more normal. It is important that you reinforce your own ability to get out with other people in your community.

Begin to care about your appearance. Start with the basics. Paint a new picture of yourself which you want the world to see. You will feel better on the inside, as well as looking better on the outside. Remember, the "inside job" will follow the "outside job." When you look better to yourself, your tears won't flow as easily and will seem out of place. Act "as if" you are okay, and soon "you will walk like you talk." Eventually when you say, "fine, thank you," you will mean it.

Gather your personal support group. It may be necessary to regroup. Confide in people you trust for your encouragement. You need all the support you can get. Be they friends, family, professional, or a formally structured group, they need to be a part of your life now. Listen to what they say to you. They care and will support you. That is why they are called your support group.

At some point, consider a really honest discussion with your beloved care person. Without manipulation of any kind, explain your needs while reassuring him of your love. Make it absolutely, one hundred percent clear that you have no intentions of ever abandoning him, and that you plan to always remain by his side emotionally, physically, and financially. But make him understand that you also need his reassurance that he will remain emotionally by your side as well. In the most tender spirit, you must explain that if you are going to be able to continue in a loving fashion as his primary caregiver, then you must be able to seek some enjoyment on your own. You may find that this conversation will have to be repeated many times, though the first time will be the hardest. This may be the most difficult task you will have to do, but it must be done if you are to feel good about moving on to the next phase of your life. It is very important that you are extremely kind, loving, and gentle. Be sincere, honest and, caring. But when you feel it is the right time, do it.

No matter what or how deeply your religious beliefs are, or even if you are not involved with an organized religious group at all, don't discount the power of prayer. Enlist your friends and family to join you in this powerful element, too. You need all the help you can get. Just a few short words at bedtime will give you a peace that will take you through the night, and your day will begin a little brighter with a spiritual inner strength connection.

# 7

# *Take Care of Yourself & Seek Help!*

Once you become ready to make concessions, new solutions will automatically enter your life and replace the problems with which you have been dealing. You must prudently reevaluate your routine and priorities and be willing to make trade-offs of things in life to which you have been accustomed. You will find that what you are releasing may not be as important to you as your newly acquired necessities. Your new lifestyle may even point out certain old financial responsibilities that have become useless habits. It will be easier for you to start eliminating things if you know their dismissal will allow you to have new, more important luxuries, such as additional help for your care person.

Seeking help of any kind is the key to your mental and physical stabilization. First, talk to your close friends and family. Remind them that "it's all in the family." Ask them for their assistance, and let them know that you need them to help you not only in a crisis situation, but in everyday living matters. Accustom them to participate regularly so that besides giving critical assistance they will feel part of your normal routine. Be honest with your potential lifesavers, and you may allow them to save your life.

If you can financially manage to hire professional caregivers, nursing assistants, or baby sitters, then do so as soon as possible. Your life will change as soon as they cross the threshold of your front door. A live-in caregiver is the most desirable choice, as he or she will take over the major duties of caring for your care person. Once again you will be fresh in the morning after sleeping through the night. Eventually you will be free to leave for awhile if you wish, and then you will find yourself recharged when you return. The responsibility of your crushing load will be dissipated. If you can't make a full commitment to a professional caregiver, at least try it out on a temporary basis. I don't know anyone that reversed their decision. Neither will you.

Take live-in help out of the luxury classification and place it in line with necessities for daily living. At the same time reverse the pattern on other commodities that you have before considered to be necessities, and place them lower on your list of priorities to make room physically and financially for your new live-in help. The willingness to change wins one more time.

Give up all of the excuses you have adhered to before. There is room in your home for an extra person. What you think is loss of privacy will actually give you more privacy, and any lack of it will not be noticed when your freedom returns. Don't wait for your care person to say that he wants a professional live-in caregiver—it will never happen. But once the professional caregiver takes over and gives your care person all of their attention, your care person will be sure that it was his idea all of the time. Yes, it probably will be a financial strain, but if at all possible—reach for it. This solution may be the most crucial one for your own survival. Neither must you allow yourself to be turned off by the frustrating exercises of teaching routines, methods, and schedules to someone new in your home. It will soon be a lot easier than struggling yourself. Even though this seems a drastic measure, it really is the easier, softer way for both of you.

Use all of your resources to assist you in finding help. Call the senior citizen center, health and care agencies, churches and synagogues, and hospitals in your area; and don't forget to use the classified ads. There are many people out of work who are happy, not only to seek employment, but to find room and board as well. The financial strain may not be as bad as you think. Negotiate. It is very important however, to screen your applicants and check all of their references closely.

Make acquaintance with a neighbor, or become friendly with a chum of your care person. Arrange for them to visit your care person, as the additional attention and new company will increase the condition of his morale. The next time you "do lunch," do it with someone that can visit your care person. Let them know they are doing him or her a great service and you will see how quickly they respond. You will rarely be turned down. While they are visiting, take a couple of hours off and get out of the house yourself. Enjoy your own lunch with a friend or do the many errands you have let slide by.

Find your privacy. No matter how small, pick a portion of your home and designate it to be yours, whether it is an entire room or even a little corner in your home—but make it "your space." Even a storeroom filled with junk can be cleaned out, freshened up, and turned into a welcome habitat with some paint, posters and a comfortable chair. Use it for your office, studio, rest area, or just a place to meditate, read, and listen to music. You only need a small area suitable for you to rest, meditate, and look out the window.

Study and understand the illness with which you are dealing. Once you are aware of the facts, some fears will be dispelled, and you will know what to expect as your situation changes. When you learn more about the disease, you will be better able to accept the progression as it occurs, and you will also gain some insight into rationally planning ahead. Don't be afraid to ask the doctor all the things you're embarrassed to ask. He's been asked them before. Make a list before you go and be ready when you are in his office. There's nothing worse than returning home from a doctor's visit and remembering the questions you forgot to ask.

The internet is also a miraculous store of information on illness. It can give you answers and enlighten you no end. Almost all illnesses have Web-sites of their own and can be easily accessed. But verify and check out the information you receive. Just because it's there on the net doesn't necessarily mean it's true and accurate. Be careful.

Take care of your own body. Get a check-up by your own physician and try to maintain a health program for yourself. Lose the extra weight you're carrying around by proper diet and exercise. A well-balanced diet is important to feed a healthy mind. A diet of excessive sugar and carbohydrates can be a killer; it can sometimes easily cause depression. Get into a fitness routine by walking and joining a gym if possible. Not only will you enjoy it physically, but your mental state will improve as well. Yoga classes are available at parks and high schools and can be a very beneficial method of health and relaxation for you. Be sure to investigate the availability of a structured meditation course. This added dimension to your life can expand your patience and tolerance level while giving you a deep sense of repose.

Take care of yourself by practicing some tender loving care on yourself. Go to the hairdresser or barber for a new look, and treat yourself to a massage, facial, manicure, and pedicure. It doesn't have to be done all at once. In fact, spreading these luxuries out will give you something to look forward to. Your confidence will increase when some of the focus is transferred to you, your life, and your needs.

Gentlemen caregivers must especially take care of themselves at this time. In the past, probably your spouse looked after all of your physical needs. Spruce up your wardrobe if you can. Find your way to a clothing store and treat yourself to a new shirt. I'll bet you haven't had anything new to wear since your wife stopped being able to shop for you. Check the sales and discount clothing stores. You will be pleasantly surprised at how much fun it will be when you get dressed up again. Don't forget, gentlemen caregivers, looking good will help your sinking confidence too.

Last, but not least, caregivers, "Just say no to defeat."

# 8

## Reach Out for Emotional Support
## Create New Interests

The further expansion and the collection of practical tools for solutions and assistance to your life's situation continues.

Once more, it is of the utmost importance to emphasize the need for you to accumulate a safe and strong support group consisting of trusting and loving dear friends and family. This is the backbone for the strength that you require at this time. These are the people who in stressful times will act for you when your energy is depleted, and love you when you are so discouraged that you feel you cannot love yourself. Surround yourself with those that you not only can count on for your emotional stability, but who you can also trust for advice on daily matters that will require decisions. It is important that they are caring enough for your welfare so while they are nurturing your soul they are not patronizing you in giving you only answers you want to hear. Their ability to be candid and not having to worry about risking your feelings for the truth is essential.

Seek help for yourself. If you feel uplifted by a support group, then use it; but exercise great care in choosing the group. You will spend a lot of time with the people in the group and you will discuss very intimate parts of your life. Therefore, you must feel you're in a safe and secure environment. Join a positively oriented, structured group led by a professional psychologist or medical personnel. Make sure that the subjects discussed deal with solutions to the issues and that they do not simply dwell on the problems. Always make sure that the group is supporting you and really not reducing your self-worth, and that you are solving problems and not taking refuge in reliving them while you are at your support group meetings. If the lump in your throat is worse at the end of the meeting, don't go back. Look further. Support groups are like individual people, so be extremely careful in selecting the group to help you. They all have different personalities, and you must find the one in which you are comfortable. However, no matter how strong you feel now, it's safer to have a support group on tap before you are in a crisis state. At that time you have neither the time nor the mental stability to go shopping for one. My favorite was the Well Spouse Foundation. Information regarding the whereabouts of the Well Spouse Foundation can be found on the internet or by calling information in your area and asking if a listing in your area exists. If not, call the nearest one and they will tell you how to locate a Well Spouse Foundation group for you. I personally recommend their philosophy. In the event there is not a meeting already set up in your area, consider starting a Well Spouse Foundation chapter in your own community. Tell them that you are interested in starting a group and they will guide you through the necessary steps. You will be doing yourself and the other caregivers in your locale a great service, and it is guaranteed that you will feel much better as you begin to help your fellow well-spouse. The excitement of starting a group will lift your spirits and give you a new positive focus in your life, and the experience for you will be greatly rewarding.

Hospitals and nursing homes are also usually a home base for support groups and a good source of information if you need suggestions and personal assistance.

If possible, enlist the aid of a professional psychologist or therapist for you to see on a one-to-one basis. Make sure you're at ease enough with this person so that you will be free to bear all of your innermost thoughts. Again, as in a support group, go shopping for the therapist with whom you find a natural rapport. Feel comfortable that he or she doesn't just sit and listen to your woes, but gives you answers that make sense. A professional therapist looks at problems from a different angle than your lay support system, and they are trained to heal your ailing mental health. Check into the possibility of Medicare or your own health insurance program to help defray the cost of a psychologist. Various insurance groups do cover such medical needs.

Find a trustworthy and loving-natured friend of your same sex with whom you can speak regularly. Ask if they have the time available for you to call daily. If you set up this pattern, you won't feel that a situation needs to be of crisis proportion before you pick up the phone. Your communication with a loving friend needs always to be available to you. Discuss everything honestly with this person, and you will find that this constant reinforcement will act as a buffer against the world. Lucky you to have a new loyal friend. Chances are they will look forward to your calls as well, and oddly enough, you will be doing them a favor by diverting their mind from their own life's difficulties. Though it may not seem possible to you now, everybody has problems.

Take the first step out into the world, thinking in a singular dimension. Create new interests for yourself, such as learning a new sport or beginning a new hobby. Consider taking lessons in painting, sculpture, or playing a musical instrument. Investigate the particular classes that pique your interest in a foreign language, music, art, cooking, business, or computers. Use your ingenuity and be inventive. The museum, art, and philharmonic groups are usually interesting and social, as well as the Toastmasters Club and Senior Citizen groups. Learn to dance and have some fun! There are an infinite amount of activities waiting for you. Instead of counting your problems at night when you are trying to go to sleep, count the different things that you would like to do. See if you can count to one hundred, and I bet you have the best night's sleep in a very long time.

The pressure of time has been removed from your life, so consider yourself in no rush at all. Neither do you have to be concerned with getting good at something, because with no clock ticking in your background, you have all the time in the world to start over if you have difficulty in whatever you are learning. What an enviable position you're in.

Please, please, please try to learn an outdoor activity, such as a sport with which you have never been involved. The fresh air is healthy and exercise is wonderful for the worried and tired heart. Sporting activities can also be the best vehicles for making new friends. Remember, the point is to create arenas for having fun, and it definitely is "okay for you to have fun!"

Engage in social interactions with people. Make new friends as well as reestablishing bonds with the old. Outside contacts are what will keep you connected to what is going on in the world, and making you feel a part of it. Bottom line here, is that you will learn to enjoy life and have fun again with people on your own.

Travel if you can. Choose fresh, unexplored destinations with new people, places, and things. Perhaps a Club-Med vacation or something entirely unlike your ordinary life will be exciting. These getaway periods will provide you time away from your care person and pressured surroundings, plus they will allow you to regain some of your physical and emotional strength. Go on that cruise alone, and dance your feet off; it's an easy method of traveling solo, because on a cruise you're never really alone. Or just lie on a lounge chair under a palm tree for a few days and listen to the gentle murmur of the ocean as you relax and discover the joys of being cared for and pampered yourself.

If you can't arrange long trips away from your responsibilities, at least take shorter excursions to nearby fun and interesting spots. Just one complete day off to the mountains or beach will be of great value to your tired soul. Pack a lunch and take everything you might need for twelve hours. Be sure you include someone to talk to. Don't go alone unless you really plan to meditate. There are many fun-filled adventures in structured hiking groups put on by local parks. Check into their availability, and you may be surprised that "right under your toes" may be a great excursion for you. When you return home you will feel as if you really have been away. Besides helping yourself, your time away from your care person will benefit him as well, as his routine will likewise be given some variety.

Think twice about pressuring your loved one into going on that trip with you because you believe that's the only way you will get to go. He probably will feel more comfortable at home with his new professional caregiver, and you may be surprised when you mention the word "trip" to your care person, and he happily says to you, "Bon Voyage." Then go, alone.

A part-time job can be a positive focus as long as you enjoy what you are doing, and are in the company of other people in a pleasant environment. Your self-worth will increase with the strokes of knowing you did a job well, and your pocketbook won't hurt from it, either. However, never lose sight of your main objective—to get out in the world with other people.

Don't "cop out" to not enjoying life by a pleading of lack of funds. Moreover, if you had to scrape up the money to buy this book and are stuck without an extra cent, then you need to use all of the tools available to you even more than the person who has a lot of extra bucks. Sadly, there can be a long time in between laughs for the financially struggling family, and you must find the courage to work on every conceivable angle that will place some quality in your life.

You will find that there are many inexpensive or free groups and classes in which you can partake, such as social, sporting, and educational groups. There are many interest groups and classes at local parks, colleges, and high schools. Churches and synagogues also offer a wonderful variety of classes and inexpensive seminars in many areas of interests and usually are focused on a social background.

Aerobics and swimming classes are healthy and social. Bridge groups, jewelry making, dance, and art classes are fun and gregarious. And group classes for sports, such as tennis, golf, karate, and fencing are available at park programs and are more fun than private instruction. In almost every community there are Senior Citizen programs that offer a variety of opportunities for classes and social functions that are a lot of fun, as well. You can begin your new socializing wherever your interest leads you. Certainly money is important, but it is not necessarily the final factor in your own recovery of the family illness.

These light solutions of getting involved with social diversions may seem like ludicrous forms of endeavors now when you haven't yet solved the many weighty issues at hand. But these tools were the main objects that kept me from being buried under my mounting problems and continued to link me to a normally functioning world. They are options for you too, and are practical suggestions that have already worked. The main thing is, that you must be willing to take part in life and get ready for your very own dance.

# 9

# Life Gets Easier with Practical Ideas

Finally, you are not alone anymore, as the National Center for Health Statistics, which is an arm for the Nation's Center for Disease Control, states in a recent survey that approximately ten million Americans have stopped their work or study because of an illness. And most everyone surveyed has a caregiver in their life.

The Act for Disabled Americans of 1990 stresses guidelines for society to follow for the betterment of the physically challenged person's life. There are multiple improvements in living, concerning work facilities, schools, offices, and job discrimination. Requirements have been mandated to upgrade and alter public buildings, stores, parks, educational facilities, and restaurants, as well as public transportation, parking, and streets for the benefit of the handicapped.

Take advantage of the points of "Handicapped Ease" that are appropriate for you:

Obtain a Handicapped placard for your automobile from your local DMV. It will provide you assistance in parking your car on public streets and parking lots and permit you to park your car closer to the entrance of buildings. Extra service in gas stations will be provided if you honk your horn and show the attendant your placard, and you will receive full service in self-serve areas in gas stations.

When dining out, notify the restaurant ahead of time that a member of your party is handicapped and requires special assistance, and watch the "red carpet" go down. Ask for whatever additional help you might need, from wheelchair assistance, special diet, or someone to accompany your care person to the restroom. Before you get inside the restaurant, ask the valet or manager to help you with the wheelchair, or simply to assist and escort you inside. I bet you won't be turned down. At the table, be sure to let someone else push your care person's chair in and out, and while they're at it, allow them to also treat you with some respect and attention too. Then, sit back and enjoy your meal.

Whether you are at a movie, theater, or sporting event, go to the front of the line. No more waiting in the hot sun or freezing in the cold night air. Just ask. In the case of the theater, inquire as to the availability of "wheelchair seats." They are usually placed in convenient locations, and I might add, they usually are located with excellent visibility to the stage.

In traveling, call your airline ahead of time and tell them that a handicapped person will be in your party. Request wheelchair assistance, and watch the envious eyes of strangers as your entire party is escorted through customs, identification check, and to the head of the line. Best of all, you won't be doing the pushing.

Find a specialty shop that sells items that are specifically designed for the handicapped. You may have to search out the whereabouts of such a store, but they do exist, and your efforts will be worthwhile. If you are fortunate to be in the close proximity of such an enterprise, you are in for a treat, as they sell items for every aspect of your everyday living. You, as well as your care person will enjoy the experience of shopping there. If you desire, request a catalog of merchandise from the wonderful specialty boutique in our area of Palm Springs. It is called "Yes I Can." It is a store complete with every imaginable item to help the physically challenged. They stock merchandise including clothing, furniture, etc. You will see items as big as chairs and sofas, and small as talking clocks. "Yes I Can" is owned and run by a lovely physically challenged woman and her husband. It is a very special place, and you can be assured that they understand the real meaning of "Yes I Can." More than likely, many of their items can be ordered on the internet or over the telephone. It's worth a try. However, if you are unable to locate a boutique that has this specialty, investigate your local hospital supply store. Often their stock is not limited to hospital or medical functions, and also has merchandise generally suited to one with special physical needs.

Investigate the availability of a day care center for the chronically ill, in your area. This will give you some breaks in your responsibility and routine, and will also add diversion to your care person's life. There are programs that can be attended on an hourly or daily basis. This again is something that you will have to search out, but certainly this could be a life saver for you at crucial times, if not on a regular basis.

Look into your eligibility of having Medicare periodically send a nurse to check the vital signs of your care person in your home. In addition, inquire as to the possibility of a physical and occupational therapist being sent regularly to give treatment to your care person by Medicare. Medicare may also send a social worker to your home to help you in your general plan of recovery for your patient. They also administer someone to periodically visit your home and bathe and massage your infirmed. Carefully check into what benefits you are allowed not only by Medicare, but by other state and national organizations. Particularly inquire as to your eligibility of receiving any benefits for custodial nursing care, either in your home or in a nursing facility.

When the appropriate time comes, look into the possibility of your being eligible for Community Hospice Care. They will be of great service, and the length of time for their services can be quite extensive, if necessary. They will see you and your loved one through the most difficult stages of illness, and will do so with the gentleness of angels.

Go shopping for a nursing facility before your care person needs one. Consider the convenience of the location, as well as the general care provided within. Return to the facility several times before passing final judgment. The first time or two may be a shock to your own emotional balance. But think of it in terms of your care person and their needs, not your healthy ones.

It is very important that you seek advice and consul from a lawyer specializing in elder law in the matter of the benefits and financial options available to you in the area of nursing, either in your home, or in a facility. You may not have to give up as much as you think. However, you need to be advised legally, as the details can be very complicated, and the alternatives can be very costly. In addition, question an attorney as to other details that may not be known as yet to you. Be sure to ask him all of the things you ever wanted to know about wills and trusts. It's always better to ask the questions before you actually need the answers.

Learn exactly what the benefits are on your supplemental health insurance policy. Don't wait for it to be too late. Study all of the details. What you don't understand, ask your agent or the company itself.

Obviously, many of these points will not remove the big problems in your life, but oftentimes the smaller ones are just as hard to handle. Hopefully, these answers will increase in size for you when you need them. And when you find yourself in need of help, remember to ASK, ASK, ASK!

# 10

## *Loneliness Ends*

You will enjoy the feeling of not being lonely anymore when you decide you are ready and willing to take the necessary steps in life that will lead you to a happier place. At some point you will get to believe that you do not have to accept everything exactly as it is handed to you. Alternatives are available that can change your destiny and cure your own debilitating disease of loneliness—and you will discover them.

Be aware of the positive changes as they take place and be willing to accept your improved self-worth as readily as you were to accept the lack of it in the past. These changes are the beginning of a whole new life for you, and each aspect of the improved transition of your body and state of mind will be very gratifying. Seize the opportunities that present themselves in your new forming lifestyle, always keeping your eyes on yourself and not on the few unimportant "gossipers" that may try to interfere with your progress.

There is neither a wrong nor right way in the matter. Once you recognize that you are fighting for your own life, you will eventually find the route that feels right for you. The main objective is to exercise your options, and make choices which will lead you out of that terrible cavity of loneliness. Take pride in your accomplishment of maintaining a life of your own while still being a caregiver to a chronically ill person, and be proud of yourself when you accidentally meet old friends while you are enjoying your new lifestyle.

As you begin to recover from your part of the illness, it will be necessary to fill the void that was left for you when depression and sadness was removed from your life. With a healthier mental state and an uplifted spirit, you will find that you will have a new abundance of time and energy. Consciously understand your changed needs as you visualize their answers, and comprehend the possibility that loneliness can be greatly reduced, if not eliminated in your life, by implementing these answers. Accept your secret yearnings and desires as possible realities, and at last give in to thoughts that your dreams of being happy again are not just irrational fantasies. Once you realize that it is possible to reshape parts of your destiny, you will shed the heavy load of resignation and you will watch your life take its new happier, natural course. No more will you have to choose between what you felt was the moral substance that held your life together with your care person, and a bit of happiness that you crave. Now you can have them both. It will become clear that in no way will your living a complete life deprive your care person of the most satisfactory existence of their capabilities.

Invite your family and friends to be supportive of your brave new life, and inform them of your need to expand your personal life. It is important that you tactfully make sure to include your care person's family as well. This may take in his children (whether or not they are your own), siblings, cousins, and parents. Remember that realistically, if they see your mental health is at stake, more than likely they will do all they can to help you. This may not necessarily be an act of mercy, generosity, or valiant kindness. The truth is, they may realize that if you break down from the strain, they could move a little closer to "the head of the line" as caregiver for their own family member. Just watch the support you receive when they understand their own vulnerability and the possibility that they may have to share their own lives, for an indefinite amount of time, with a chronically ill person. In the long run, you win again; you need all the support you can get, from friends and family alike.

At the beginning, devise a schedule for your free time based on your care person's needs. Allow quality time with your care person when they are awake and active, and then take time for yourself when they are resting. Eventually, your confidence will build to a point that you will use your own needs and appointments as your cue for your own relief, as long as you always make sure your plans do not interfere with the needs of your care person. Once you build up your new social life, you will use your calendar to decide when you stay and when you go. What fun it will be when you learn that calendars are not only for doctor's appointments, but are for parties, classes, luncheons, etc., etc., etc., etc., etc., etc., and ETC. However, you must never get so addicted to your new-found life, that you can't say "no" to pleasure if your care person really needs you. He comes first and foremost in your life. Always be accessible in case you are needed. This not only will provide protection and confidence for your care person, but you also will be able to relax and enjoy yourself, knowing no crisis is occurring in your absence. You have choices now, and you no longer need to ask "Is it all right if I go?" Within these parameters, it is. Just be sure that you are always in control.

Communicate with your care person, reassuring him that he knows he is still your main focus in life but that your happiness is now important as well. Share with him as many of your new interests as possible, without making him feel left out. In time, you will learn to go farther away, and at the same time, he will be drawn closer to you. Soon he will be on your side in the success of your new accomplishments, endeavors, and even happy for the friends that you are making. Ask your friends, new and old, to come to your home and visit with you and your care person. Don't be afraid to make a party around the holidays. Everyone likes to go to parties. It is an excellent time to bring some frivolity into your home. Your friends will be kind and solicitous as they will understand your situation—and your care person will ultimately benefit as he will be having additional company.

You must be very careful with your care person's feelings. Always try your hardest to protect their feelings of rejection, embarrassment, and inadequacies. Even though you need to talk honestly with your care person, edit carefully what you say, reassuring him of your love and that you will not leave him. You may be afraid of a conversation of this sort, but this open verbal communication will actually be a great tool to use to bring the two of you back to feeling a closeness from which you drifted a long time ago. This will help bring you on the same side of the team. Remember, there is only one.

The time has come for you to take some emotional risks. You can handle them. The next time someone says to you, "What about dinner?" Remember how hungry you are; you haven't enjoyed a meal in years. The answer to the question is easy. It is "yes." Keep in mind that dinner doesn't necessarily also mean "breakfast."

Acknowledge your need to make friends with persons of the opposite sex, and trust that your need will automatically take place when it is supposed to. You will know when that is. Maybe it is now. Place yourself in social and business environments where you can meet new people. Never cease remembering that you are looking for what you are looking for—a companion, and friend. Once you find those qualities in a person, you may just lighten up. It doesn't have to be all that serious. Even though "no pain—no gain," pain is not fun, and you have had your share. Keep in mind that you're definitely not looking for someone to replace your spouse. You already have one that you intend to keep.

Though loneliness may be the element that can lead to a more fulfilling life, it can also be so powerful as to lead one in the wrong direction. It is imperative that one avoid any unnecessary rejection or hurt that can arise when risking the emotional state of any new friendship. It is only possible to establish genuine rapport and friendship with someone you feel you can genuinely trust. Having these standards and requirements in mind you will then find that an individual with these features can be capable of generating the warmth and understanding in the gentle manner that you require.

Even though this book has been written by a middle-aged woman, I feel secure in saying that the feelings, insights, and suggestions are not limited to one sex or age group. The feelings that led to my solutions do not have boundaries; nor does the courage for the solutions. If you are a male caregiver, the answers are exactly the same. In fact, perhaps the urgency you are feeling may be more acute, as your masculinity and normal sense of responsibility are involved. Helpless though you may feel, the need for release from your sense of entrapment is the same as for anyone else.

If you are in the growing category of a caregiver for a parent, take heed of the information here. It pertains to you. Your own life as well must be cared for. Because the innocent demands of a parent can be overwhelming and never-ending. They can't help it. They need your help. But know the value of your own life, and don't forget to live it with great value.

# 11

## *Acceptance and Survival*

Even though my struggle for survival lasted sixteen long years, ultimately I did survive. It doesn't matter how long you have been struggling in the syndrome of your caregiving ailments, you also can recover at any point you choose. You don't have to wait or suffer as long as I did, and hopefully you won't. Neither must you be a pioneer in the field of this journey, as the trailblazing has already been done. The only pity will be if you don't start at all. As in many illnesses, the sooner one begins medical, physical, or emotional treatment, the sooner will one enjoy restored health. Can't you imagine how quickly your care person would jump at the chance to try a tested procedure for the cure of his ailing body? Of course you can. And so must you, for the fight for your own survival.

# Epilogue

Three years after the passing of my dear husband Chester Breskin, I married the handsome dancer with whom I did the Western Two-Step in this book. But again, as fate would have it our marriage was short-lived by just four years as Don Clarke died of a sudden heart attack at the age of 67.

Bereavement was again forced upon me, but with the lessons that I had learned I was fortunate to meet the man whom I have been happily married to for the last 15 years. The years have flown by with a rapid pace and I am now well into my senior years and still enjoy an active social life, golfing, and of course, an occasional dance.

Lightning Source UK Ltd.
Milton Keynes UK
UKHW010631080822
406998UK00001B/76

9 781958 678091